MESSAGES OF

Inspiration from the Holy Bible

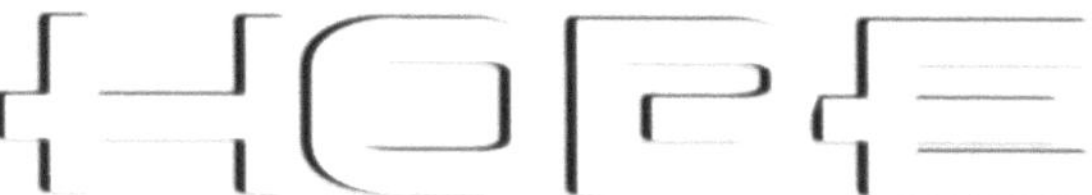

MESSAGES OF HOPE - INSPIRATION FROM THE HOLY BIBLE

Premier Edition Published in 2015 in the United States of America

Sources: All Bible verses paraphrased from a multitude of various scriptures including: the Geneva Holy Bible, New King James, The Torah, Catholic Public Domain, Orthodox Jewish Bible, NIV Anglicized, among many others.

WWW.MYDOVESONG.COM

ISBN-13: 978-0615977812
ISBN-10: 0615977812

MESSAGES OF

INSPIRATION FROM THE HOLY BIBLE

HOPE

D. ASHANTI-
DUBOIS

My Dove Song
MYDOVESONG
PUBLISHING

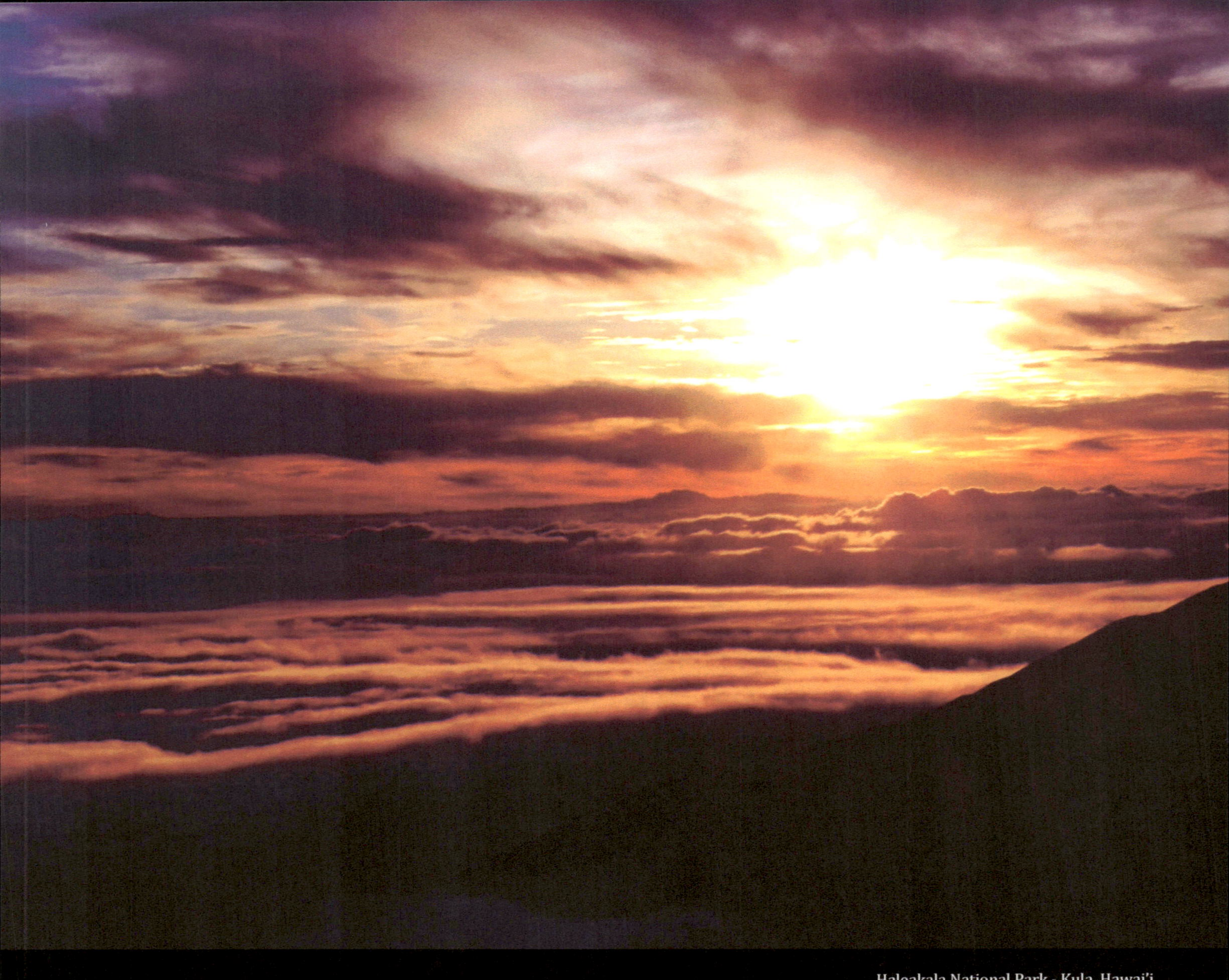

Haleakala National Park - Kula, Hawai'i

Isaiah 49: 15-16

The Divine will never forget you...

"...But Zion says, 'The Lord has forsaken me; my GOD has forgotten me.' Can a woman forget the infant at her breast, or a loving mother the child of her womb? Even these forget, but I will not forget you. Your walls are always before my eyes, I have engraved them on the palms of my hands."

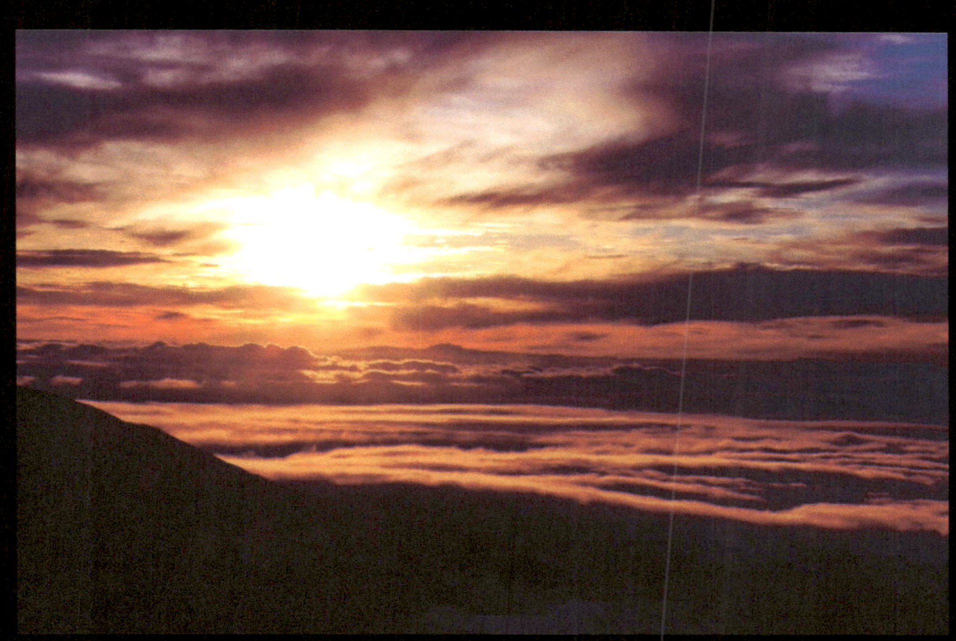

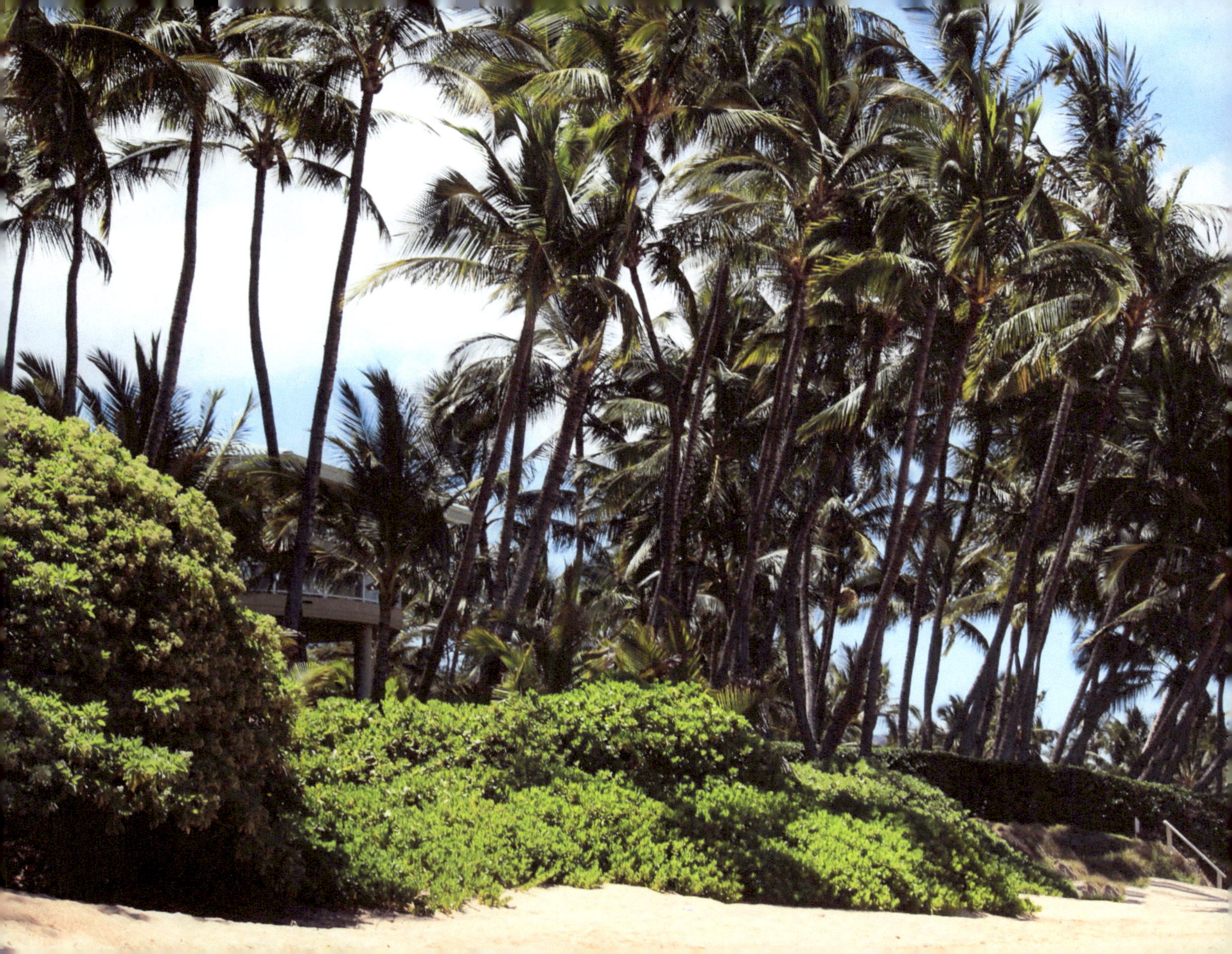

2 Timothy 1:7

The Divine has given you power...

"...For GOD has not given us the spirit of fear, but of power, love, and of a sound mind."

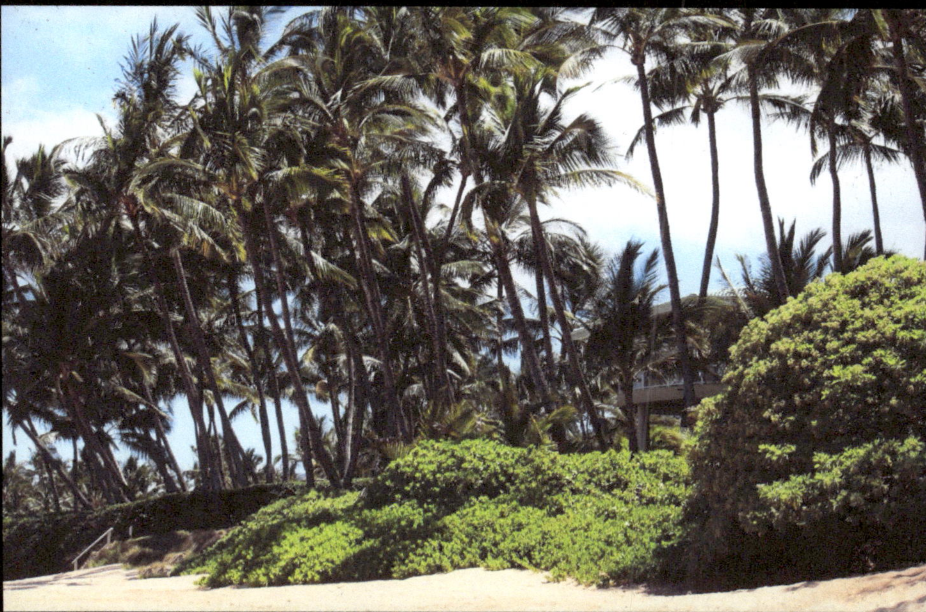

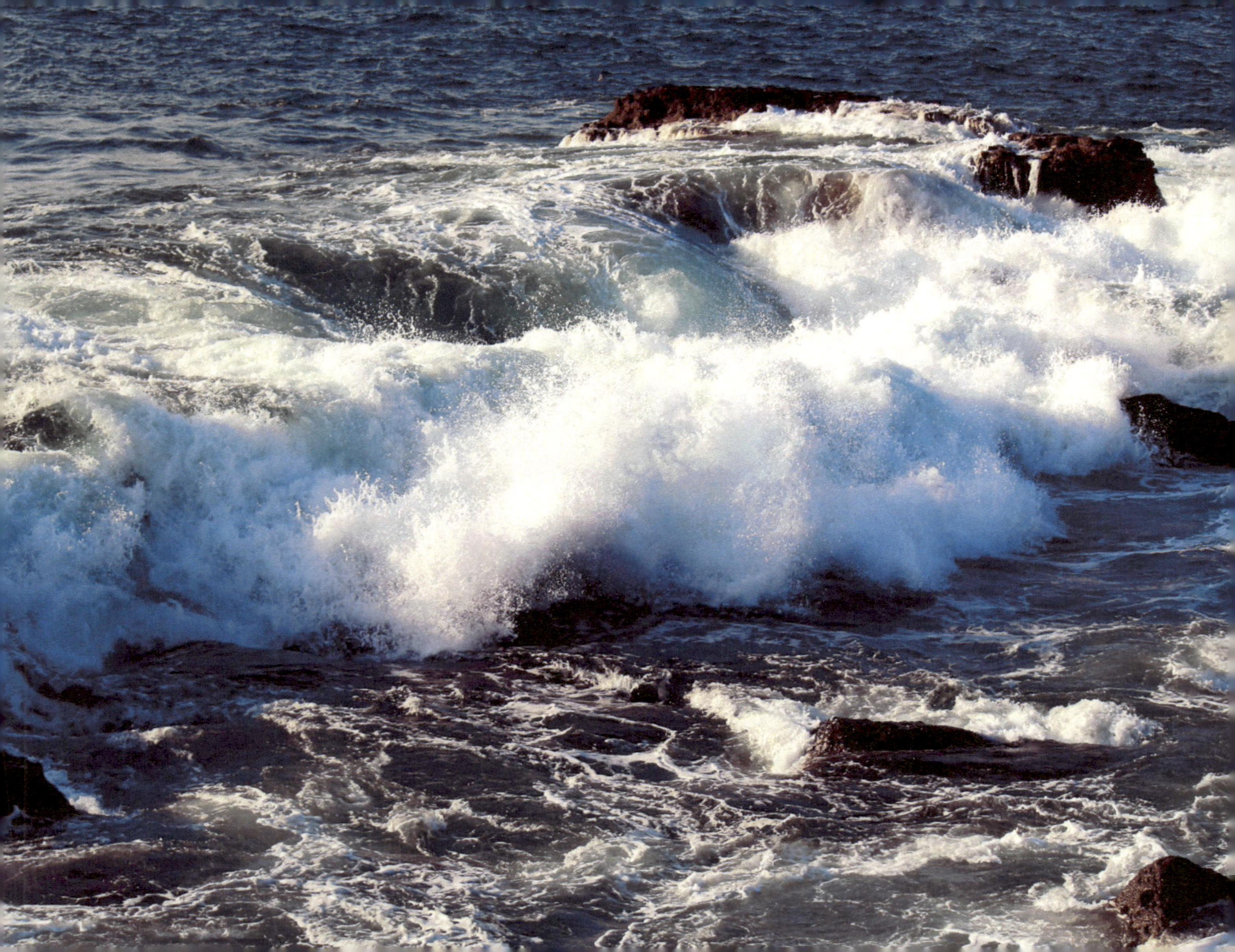

Hebrews 10: 32-36, 39

Have confidence even when you have suffered loss...

"...You met the challenge of great suffering and held firm. Some of you were abused and tormented to make a public show, while others stood loyally by those who were so badly treated. And you had compassion on me in my chains, and cheerfully accepted the seizure of your possessions, knowing that you possessed something more lasting in Heaven. Then do not throw away your confidence, for it carries great reward. Because you need patience, so after you have done the will of GOD, you may receive what He has promised. ...We are not among those who shrink back and are lost; we have the faith to make life our own."

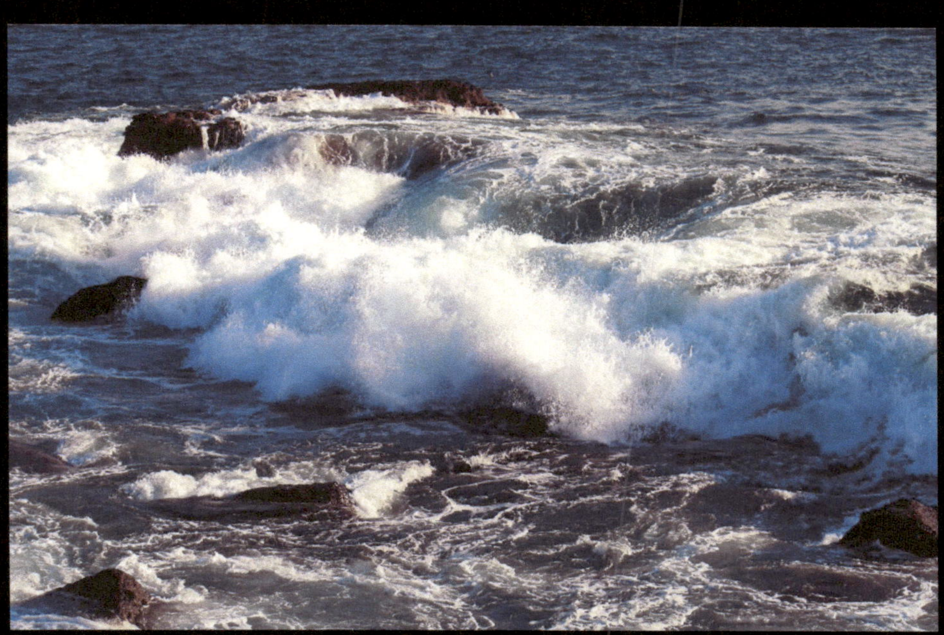

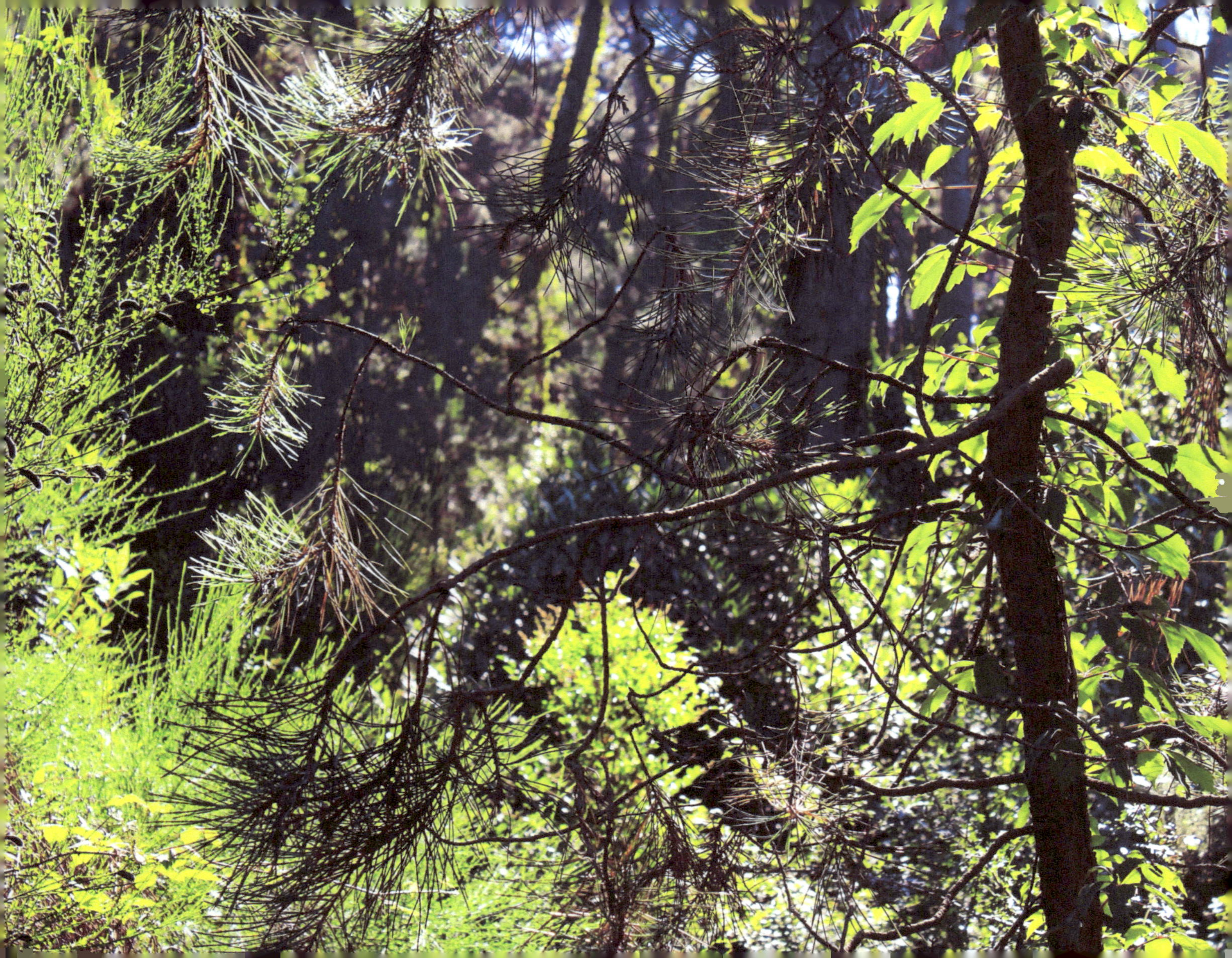

Mathew 5: 3-10

When you love The Divine, you are blessed beyond words...

"...Blessed are those who know they need GOD; for theirs is the kingdom of heaven. Blessed are they that mourn; for they shall be comforted. Blessed are the gentle in spirit; for they shall inherit the earth. Blessed are those who hunger and thirst to see right prevail; for they shall be satisfied. Blessed are they who show mercy; for they shall receive mercy. Blessed are the pure in heart; for they shall see GOD. Blessed are the peacemakers; for they shall be called the children of GOD. Blessed are those who are persecuted for righteousness sake; for theirs is the kingdom of Heaven." - (Jesus Christ)

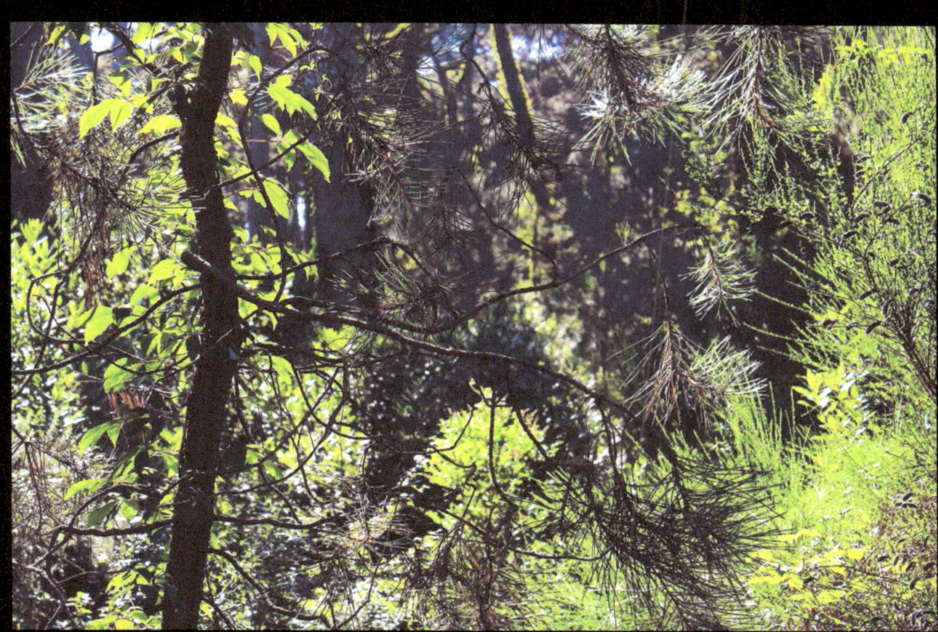

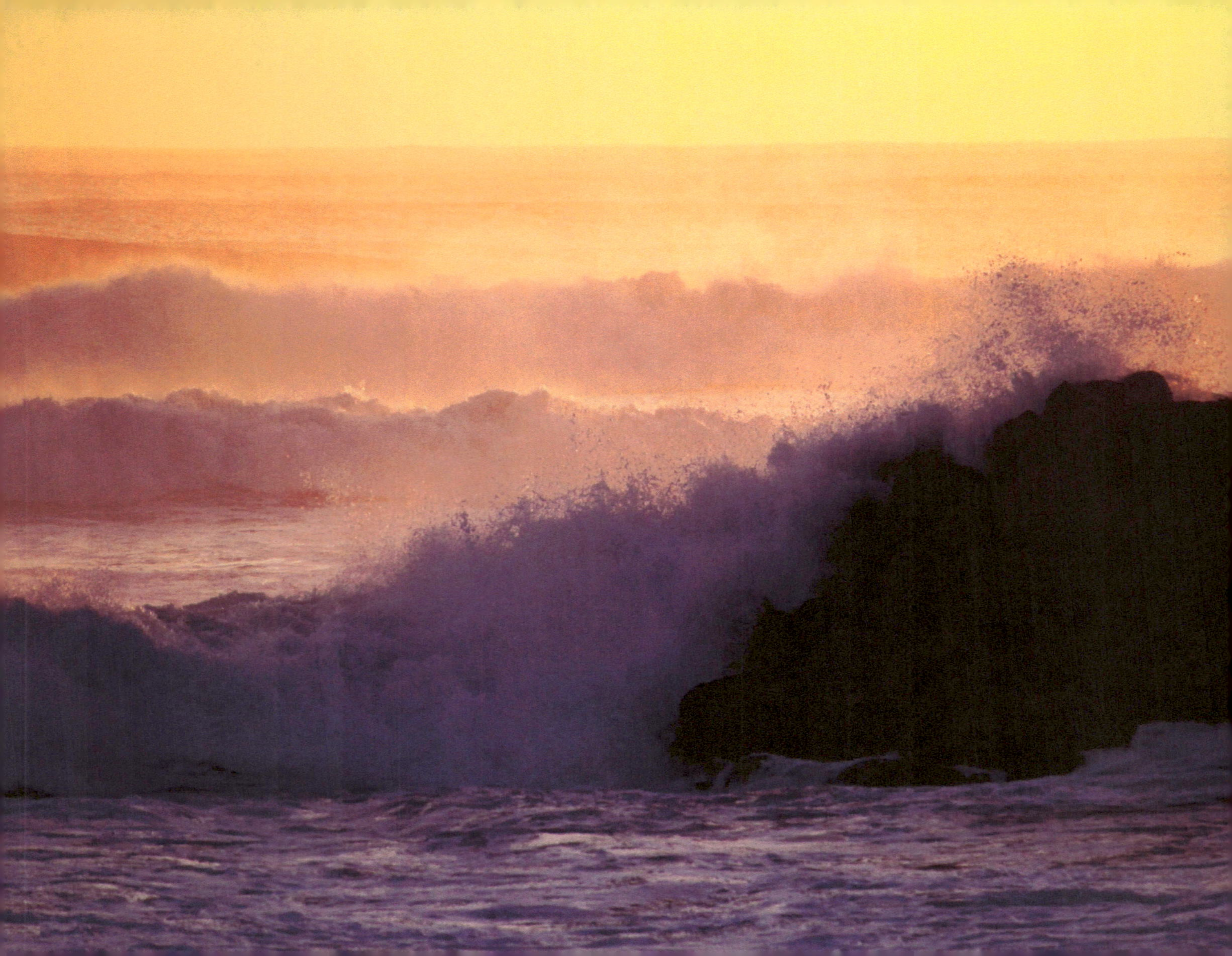

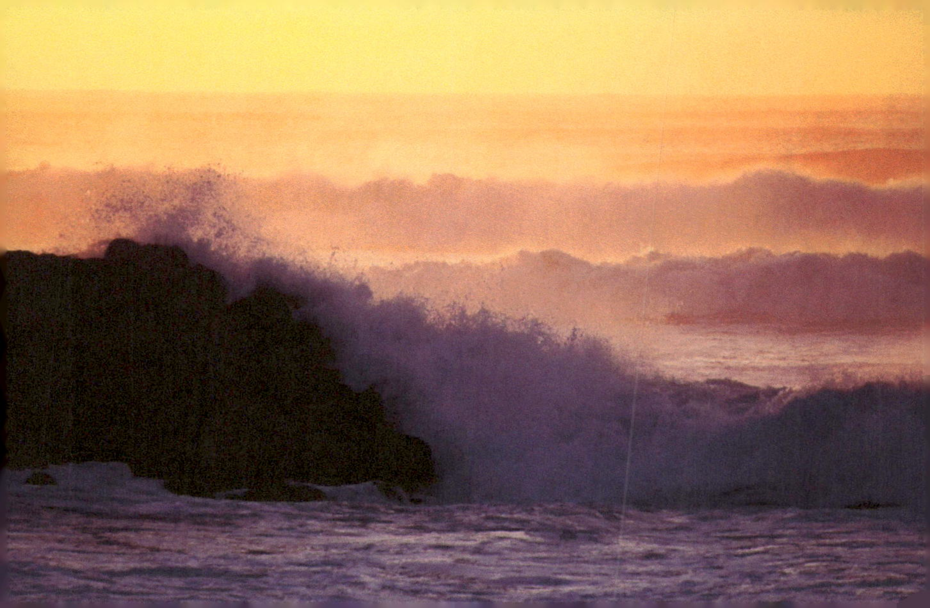

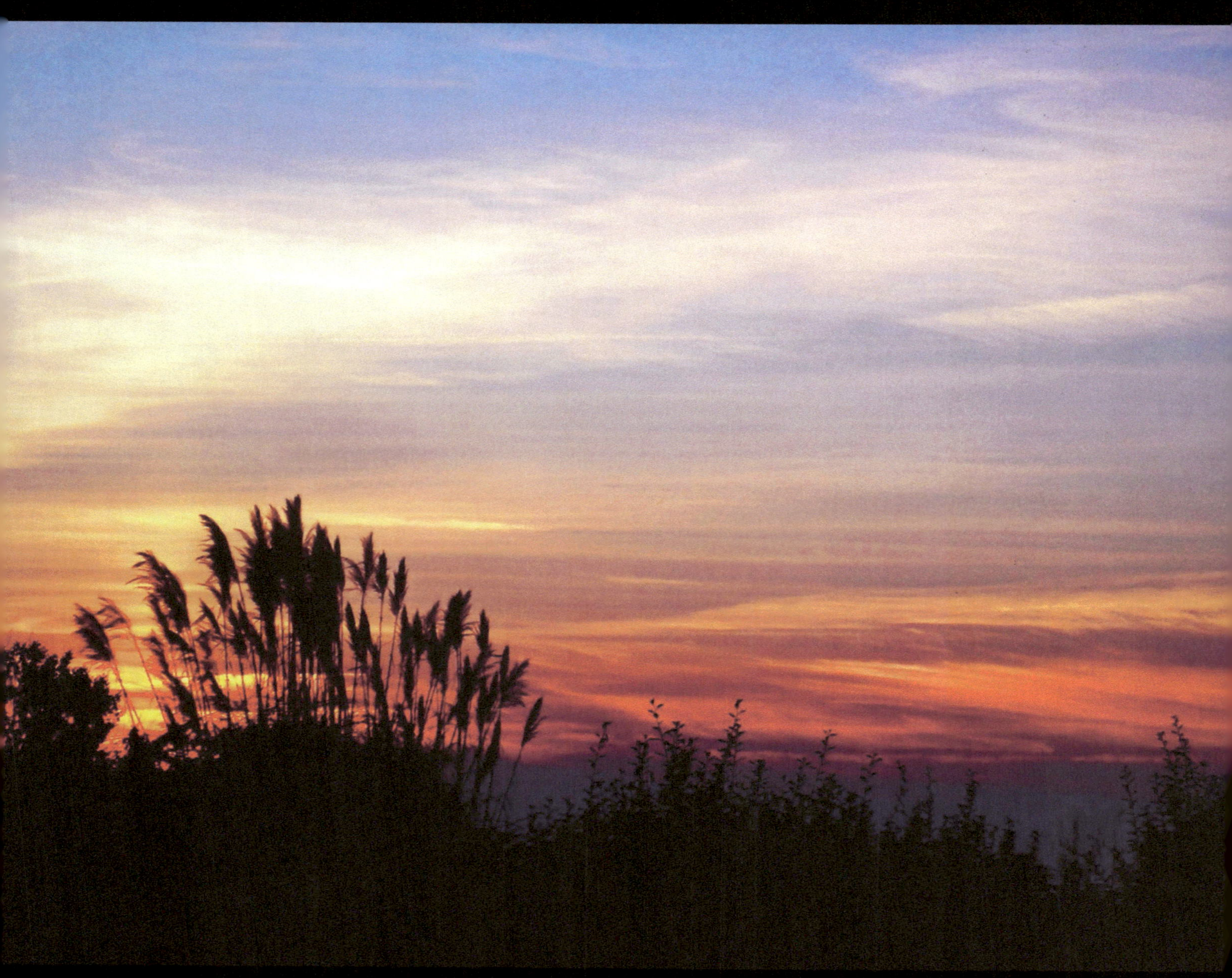

Sunrise Chiberta - Anglet, France

1 Thessalonians 5:16-18

No mater what happens in your life, whatever you are going though, rejoice.

Pray without ceasing through every storm and every drop of rain.

There is a miracle in keeping your faith. This is what GOD wants for your life. Be positive.

"Rejoice always. Pray at all times, because this is what GOD wants from you during your life, when you believe in Yeshua, Christ Jesus."

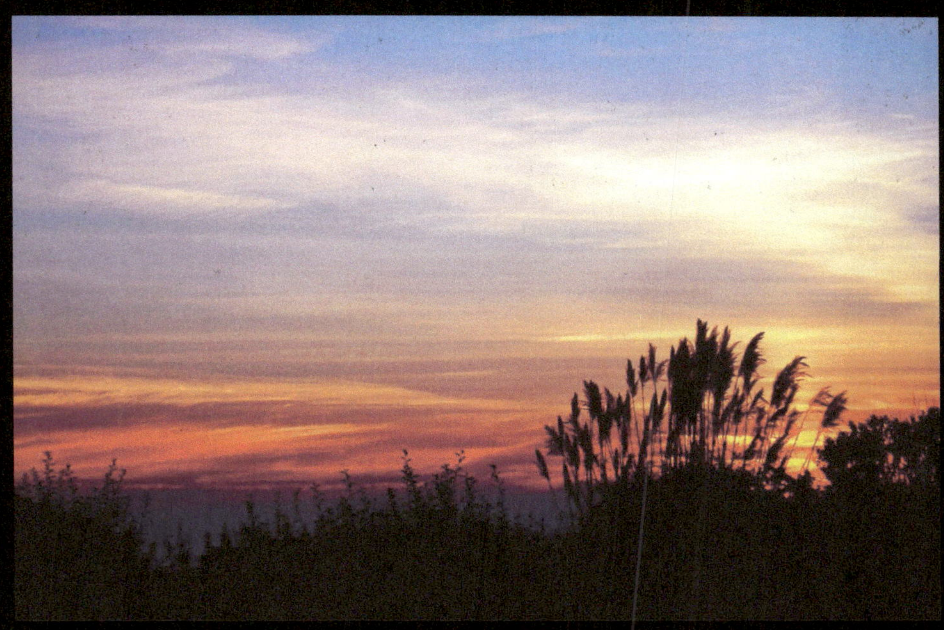

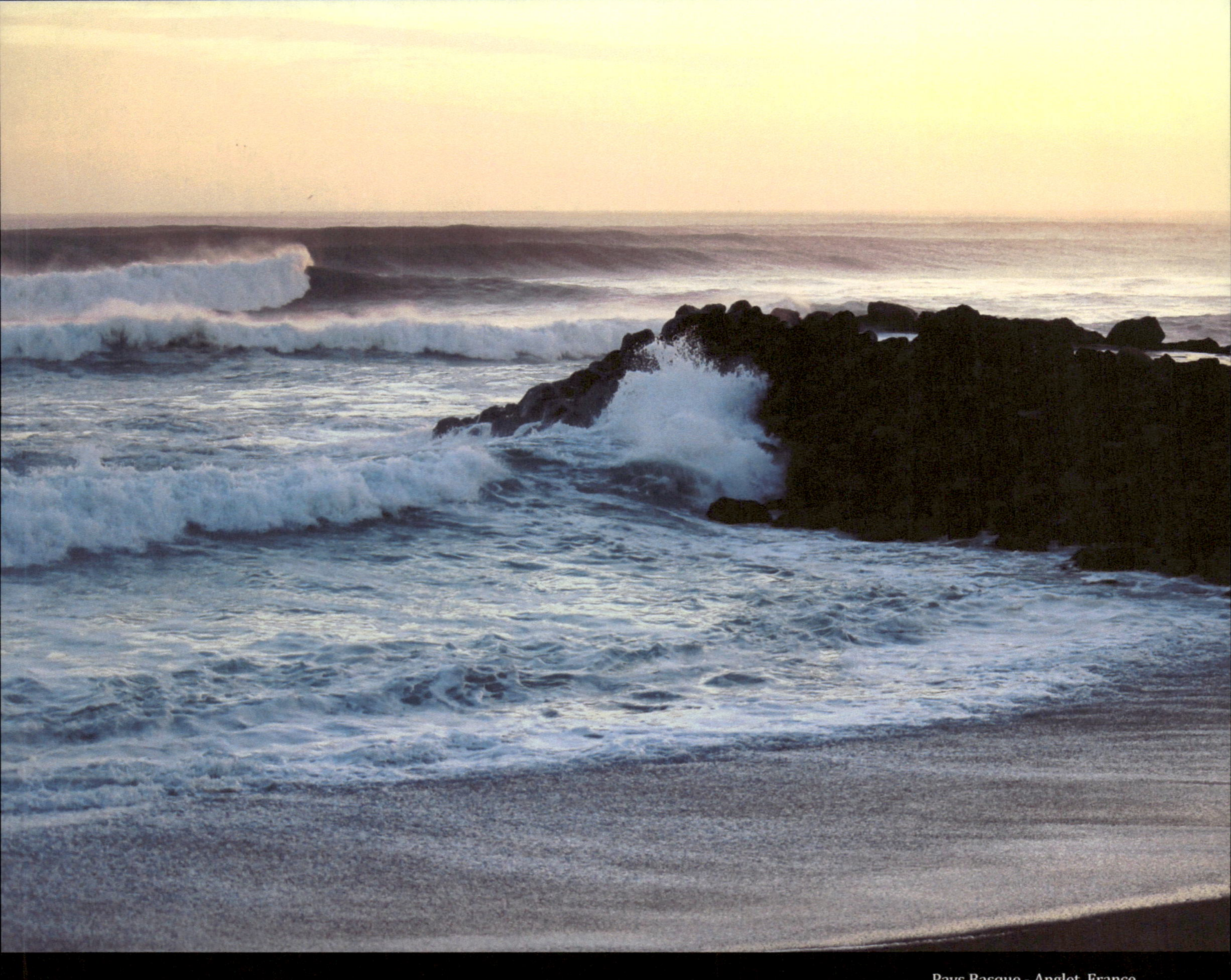

Pays Basque - Anglet, France

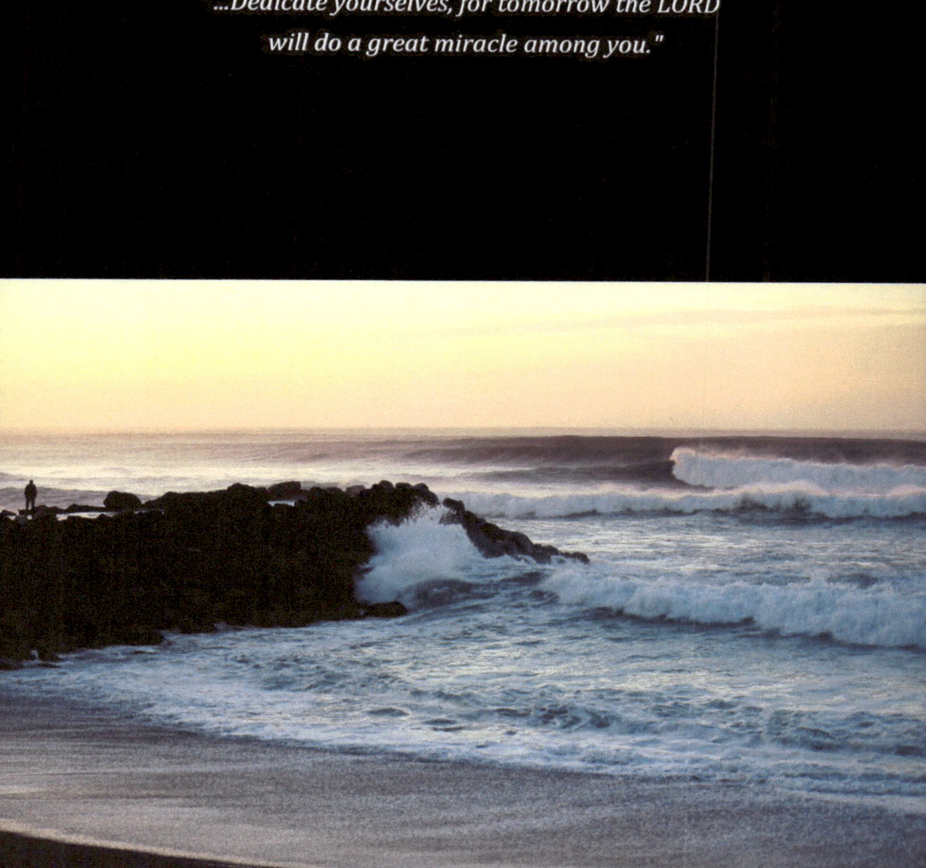
"...Dedicate yourselves, for tomorrow the LORD
will do a great miracle among you."

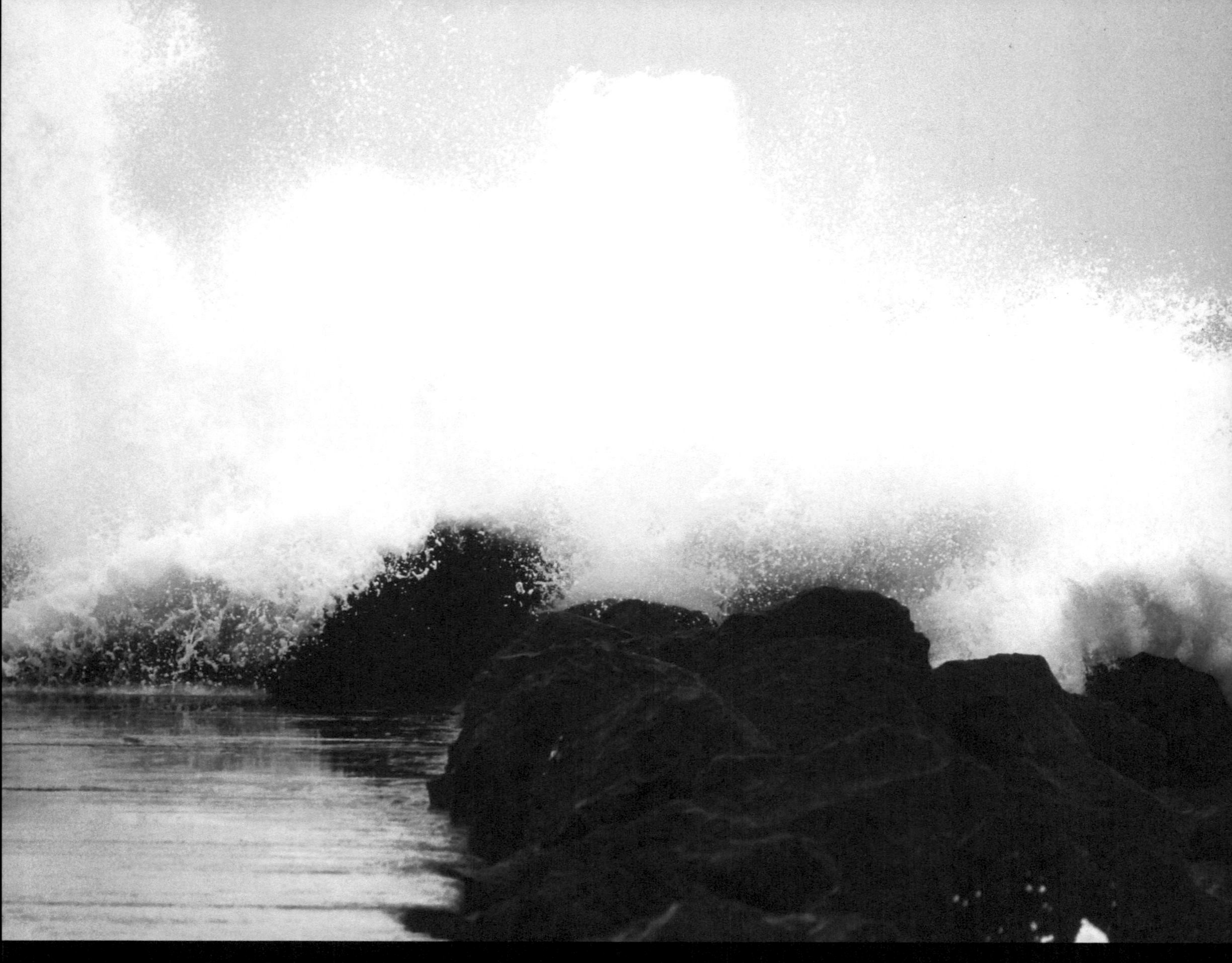

Chambre d'Amour - Anglet, France

Psalms 46:1-3

In the midst of trouble, call on the Divine and do not be afraid.

God is your hope. Have faith.

"GOD is our hope and strength, and our help in times of trouble. Therefore, we will not be afraid, though the earth trembles and the mountains tumble into the midst of the sea, and the oceans rage and toss, and the mountains quake from their thunderous rage."

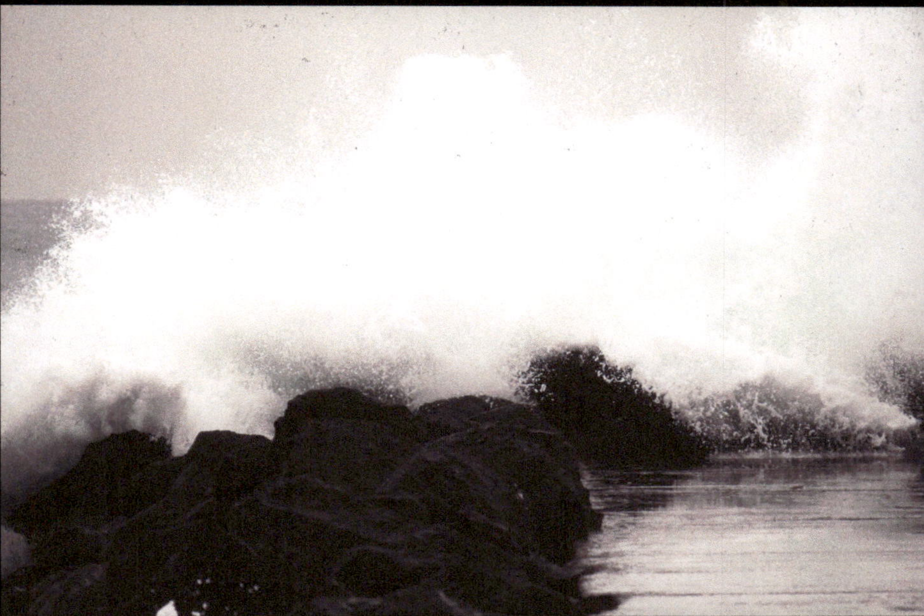

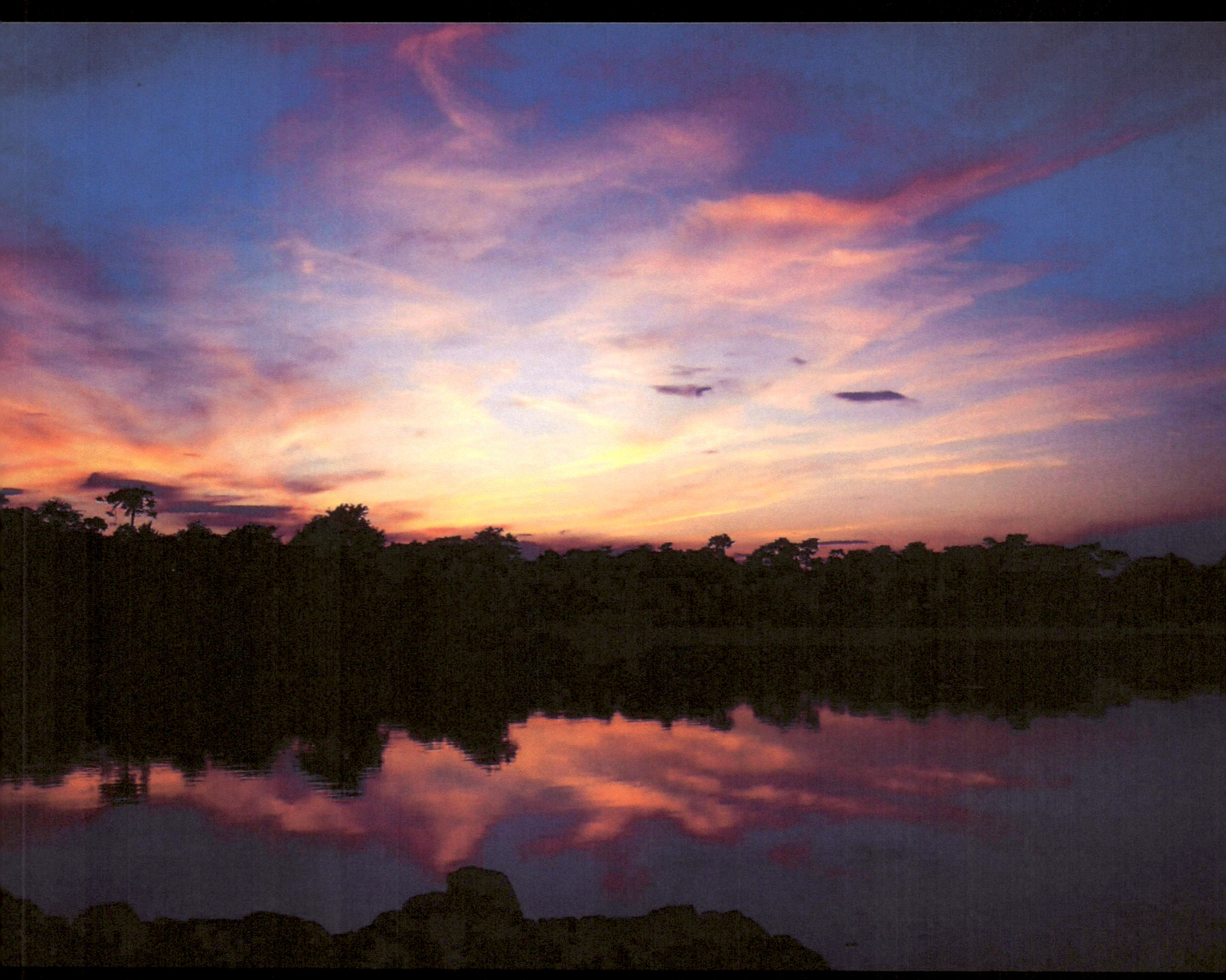

Sunset in Hossegor- Pyrenees Atlantique,

Mathew 7:7-11

The Divine will give you everything that is good for you.
Ask for what you want.

"Ask, and you shall receive; seek, and you shall find; knock, and the door shall be opened. For everyone who asks receives, he who seeks finds, and to him who knocks, the door shall be opened. Is there a man among you who will offer his son a stone when he asks for bread, or a snake when he asks for a fish? If then, as bad as you are, know how to give your children what is good for them, how much more will your heavenly Father give good things to those who ask Him!"

(Jesus Christ)

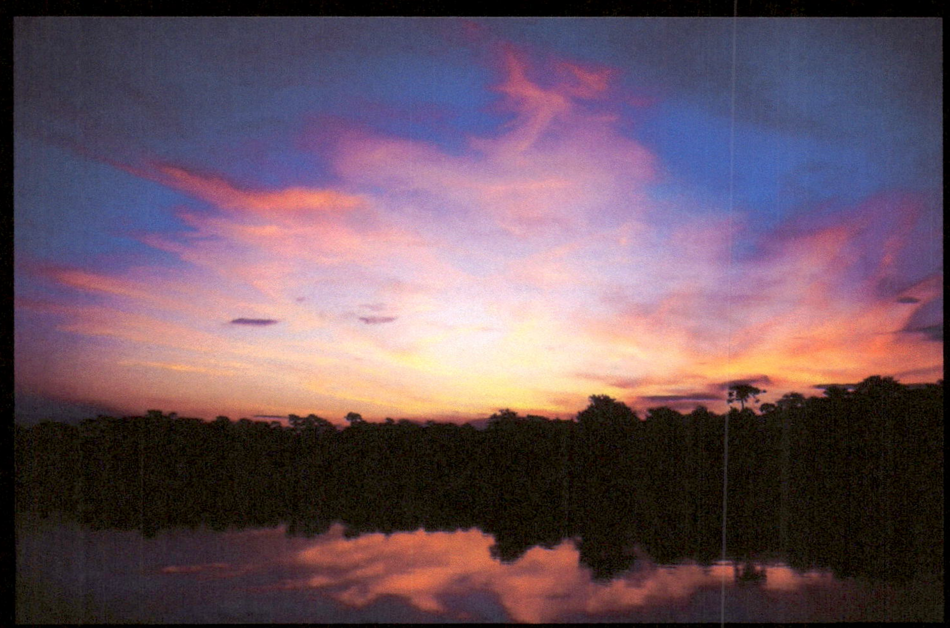

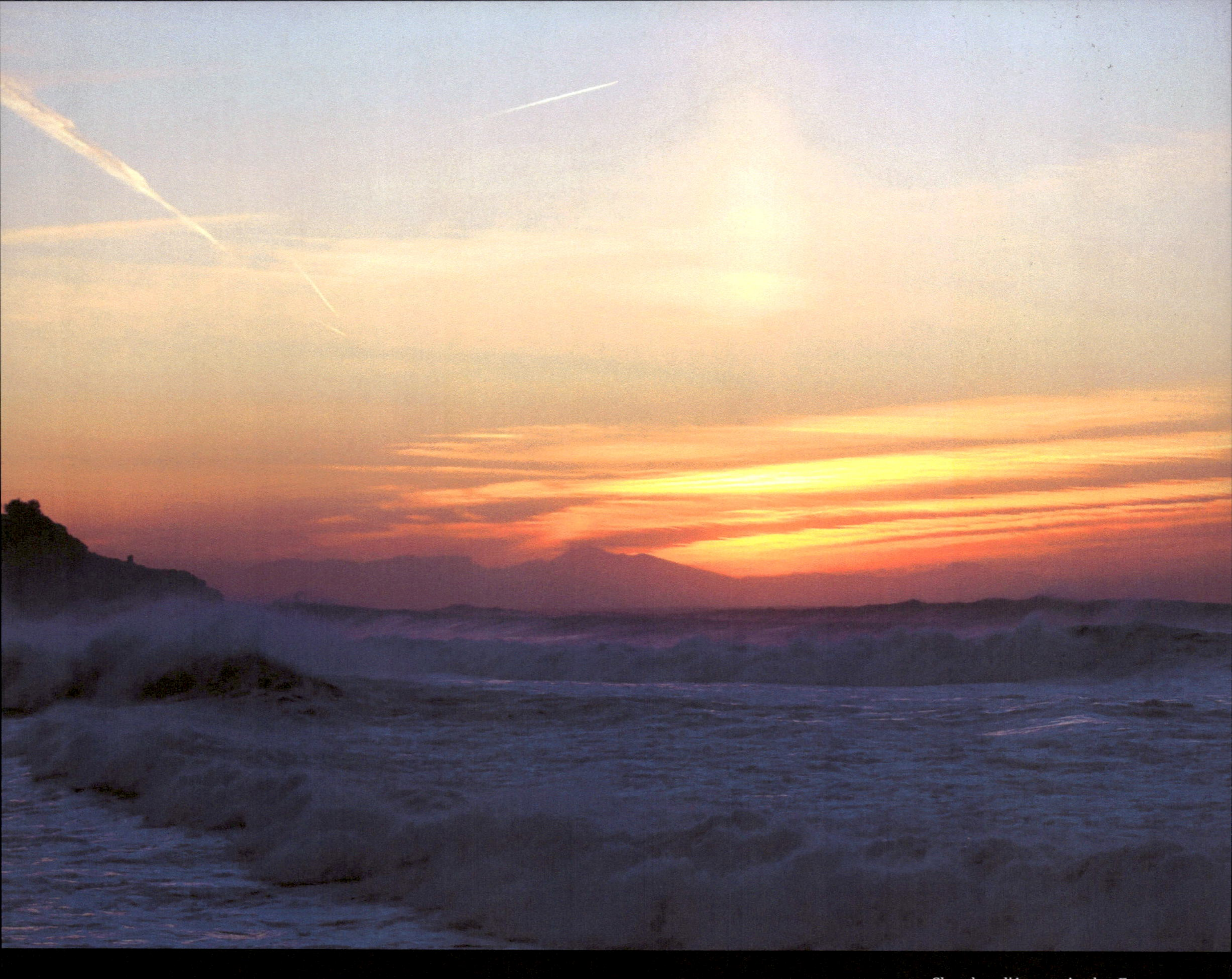

Chambre d'Amour Anglet, France

The Divine will provide all of your needs.

"...I tell you, do not worry about your life, what you will eat, or what you will drink: nor about your body, or what you will wear. Is life more than just eating, how you look or feel? Is it more than clothes? Look at the birds in the air... They do not work in the fields for money nor store food in pantries, yet your Heavenly Father feeds them. Are you not worth more than birds? ...Why worry about clothes? Consider how the lilies grow in the fields; they do not work, they do not weave; and yet, I tell you, even Solomon and all his luxuries was not dressed like one of these. But if that is how GOD clothes the grass in the fields, which is there today, and is thrown in the oven tomorrow, then will he not all the more clothe you? How little faith you have! No, do not worry and ask, 'What are we going to eat? or, What are we going to drink?' or, 'What will we wear for clothes?' ...Your Heavenly Father knows that you need all of those things. First search the kingdom of GOD, and all that is just and right; and all these things shall be given to you. Therefore, don't worry about tomorrow; because tomorrow will look after itself. Each day has enough problems of its own." **(Jesus Christ)**

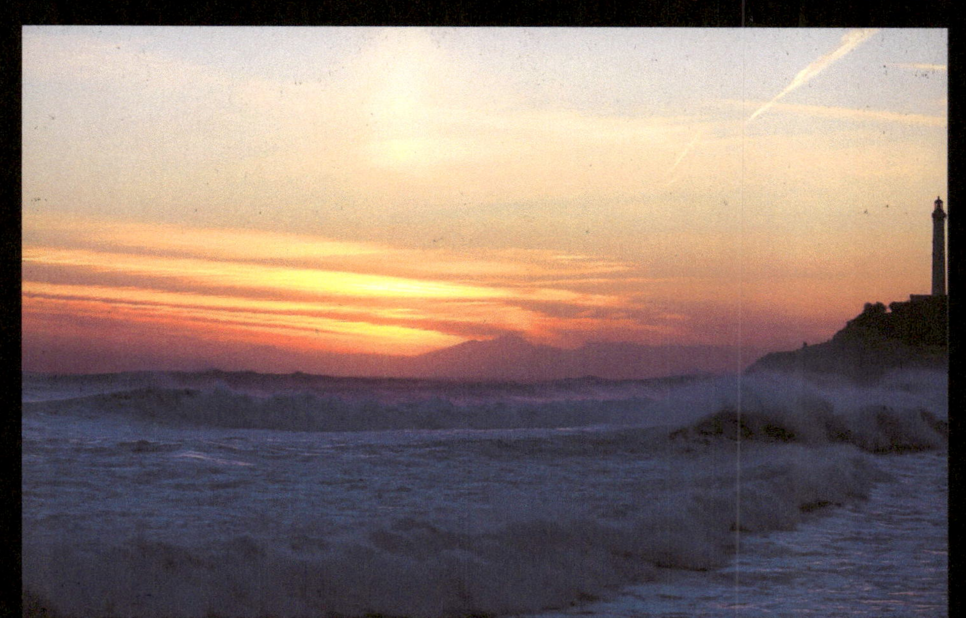

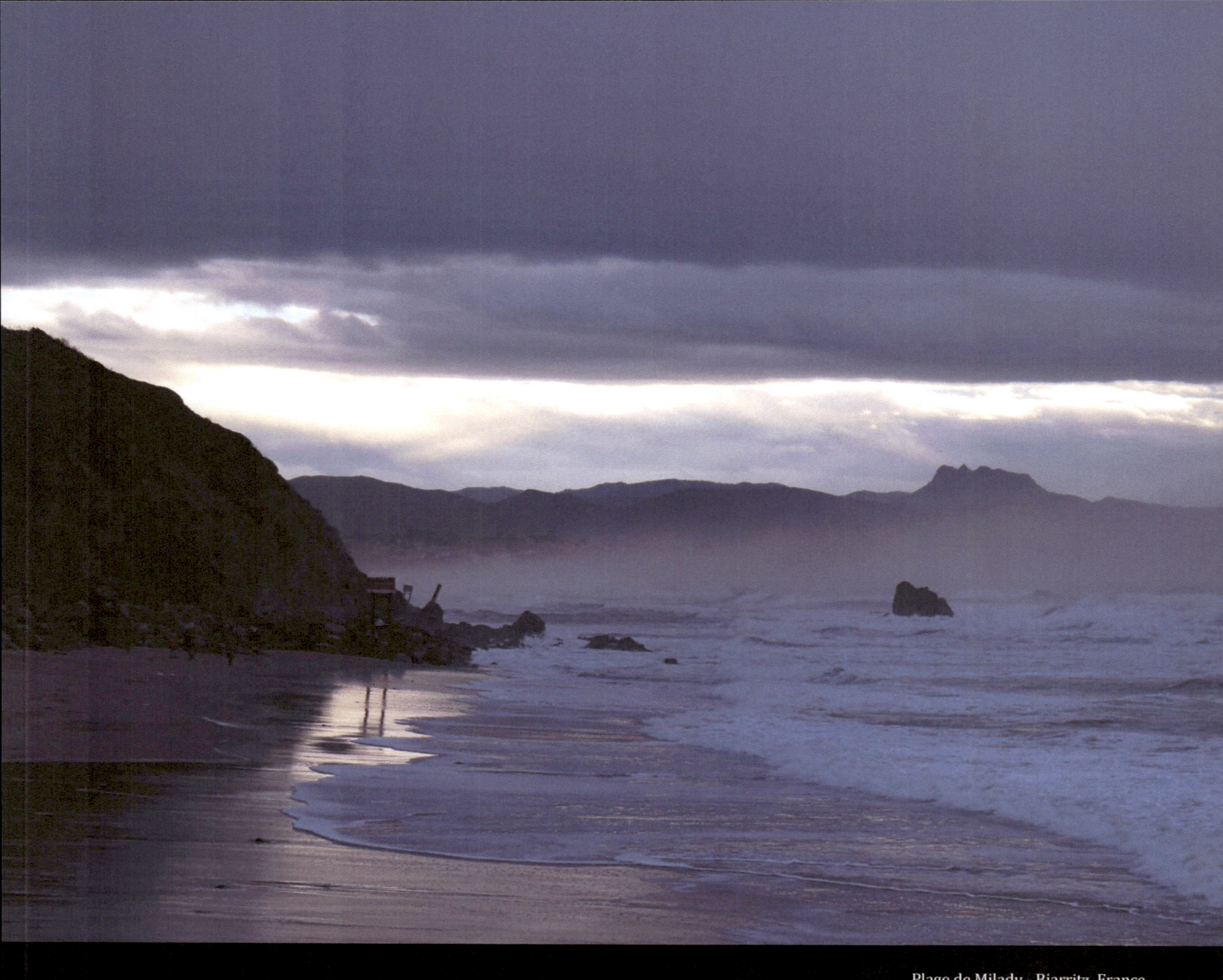

Plage de Milady - Biarritz, France

When they came to the gate of the city, there was a young man being carried out who had died. He was the only son of his mother who was a widow and many people from the city was with her. And when the Lord saw her, he had compassion for her. He said to her, 'Don't cry'. Then he went over and touched the stretcher; the men who was carrying it stopped. Then he said, "Young man, arise." And the woman's son sat up and began talking. (Jesus) then gave him to his mother.

(Jesus Christ)

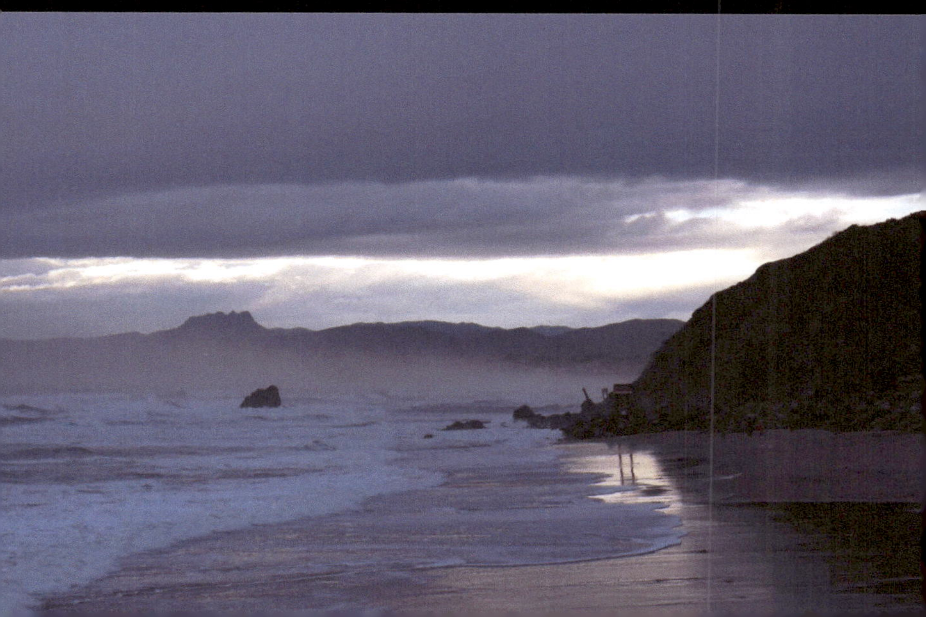

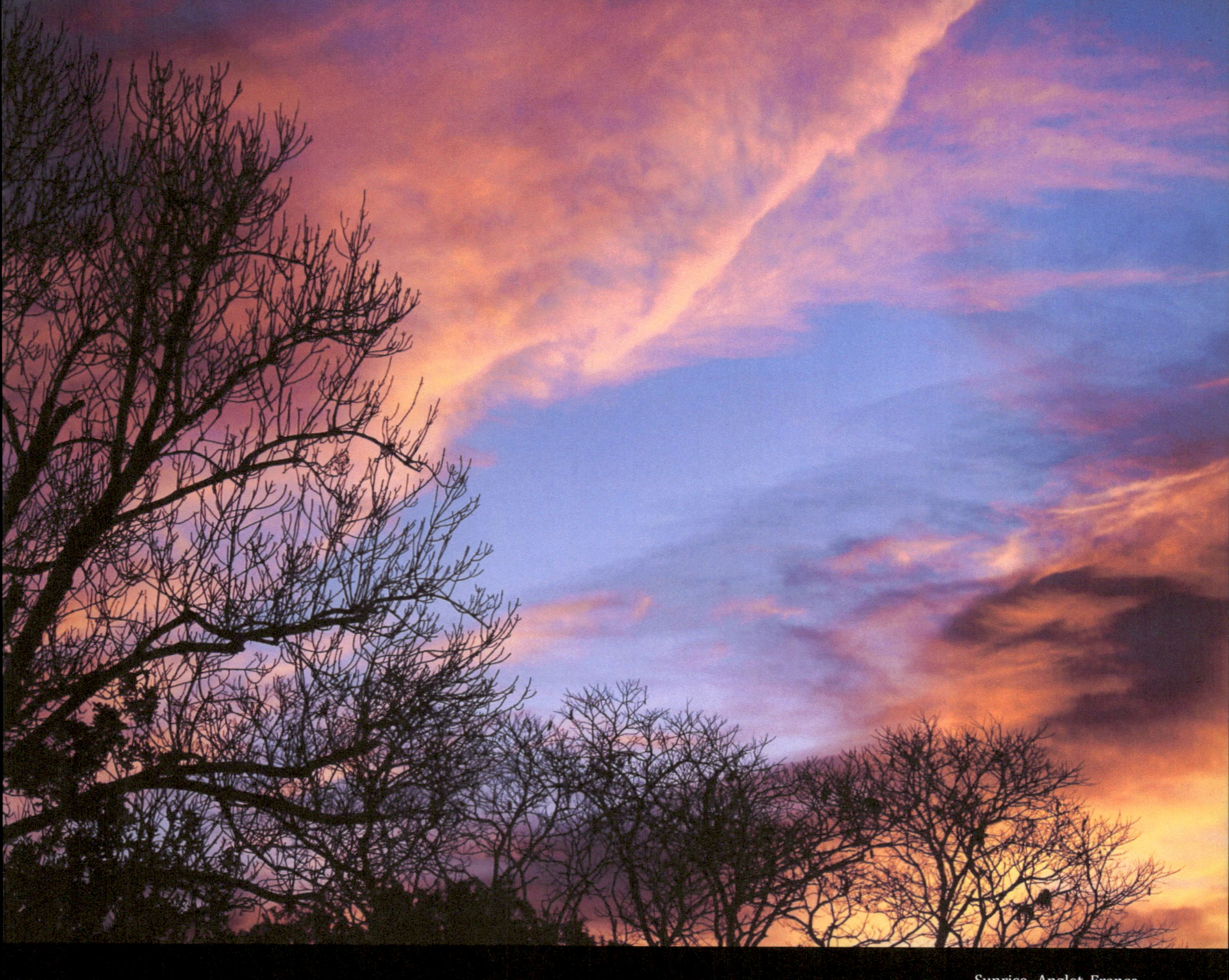

Sunrise -Anglet, France

Psalms 23

The Divine will guide and protect you.

GOD will provide your every need.

"The LORD is my shepherd, I shall not want. He makes me to lie down in green pastures. He leads me beside the still waters. He restores my soul. He guides me on the path of righteousness for His name's sake. Even if I walk through the valley of shadows and death, I will fear no evil; for You are with me. Your shepherd's rod and staff protect me. You prepare a table before me in the presence of my enemies. You anoint my head with oil; my cup runs over. Surely, goodness, and mercy shall follow me all the days of my life, and I will dwell in the house of The LORD forever."

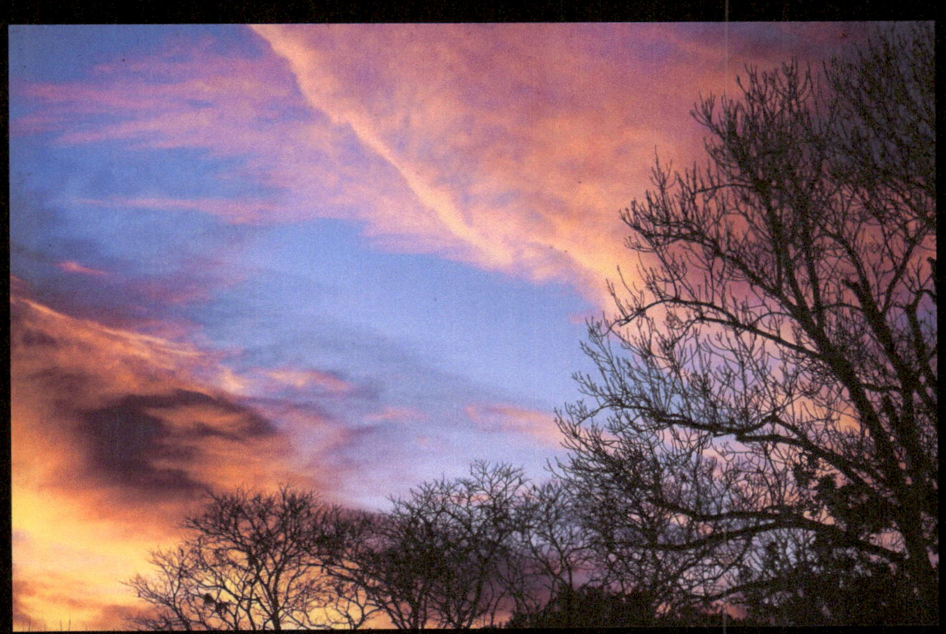

View from LaRhune, Pays Basque, France

Psalms 121:1-2, 4-8

The Divine helps you.

He will guard you body and soul.

"If I lift up my eyes to the hills, where shall I find help? My help comes only from The LORD, maker of Heaven and earth. The LORD will never slumber nor sleep. The LORD is your guardian; your defense at your right hand. The sun shall not strike you by day, nor the moon at night. The Lord will protect you against all evil; He will guard you, body and soul. The LORD will guard your going out and your coming in, now and for evermore."

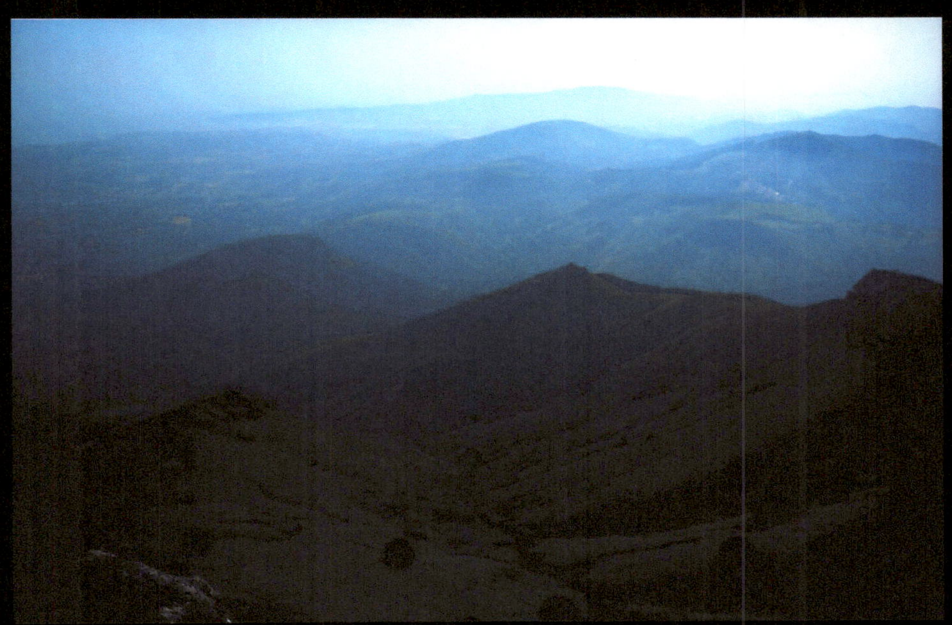

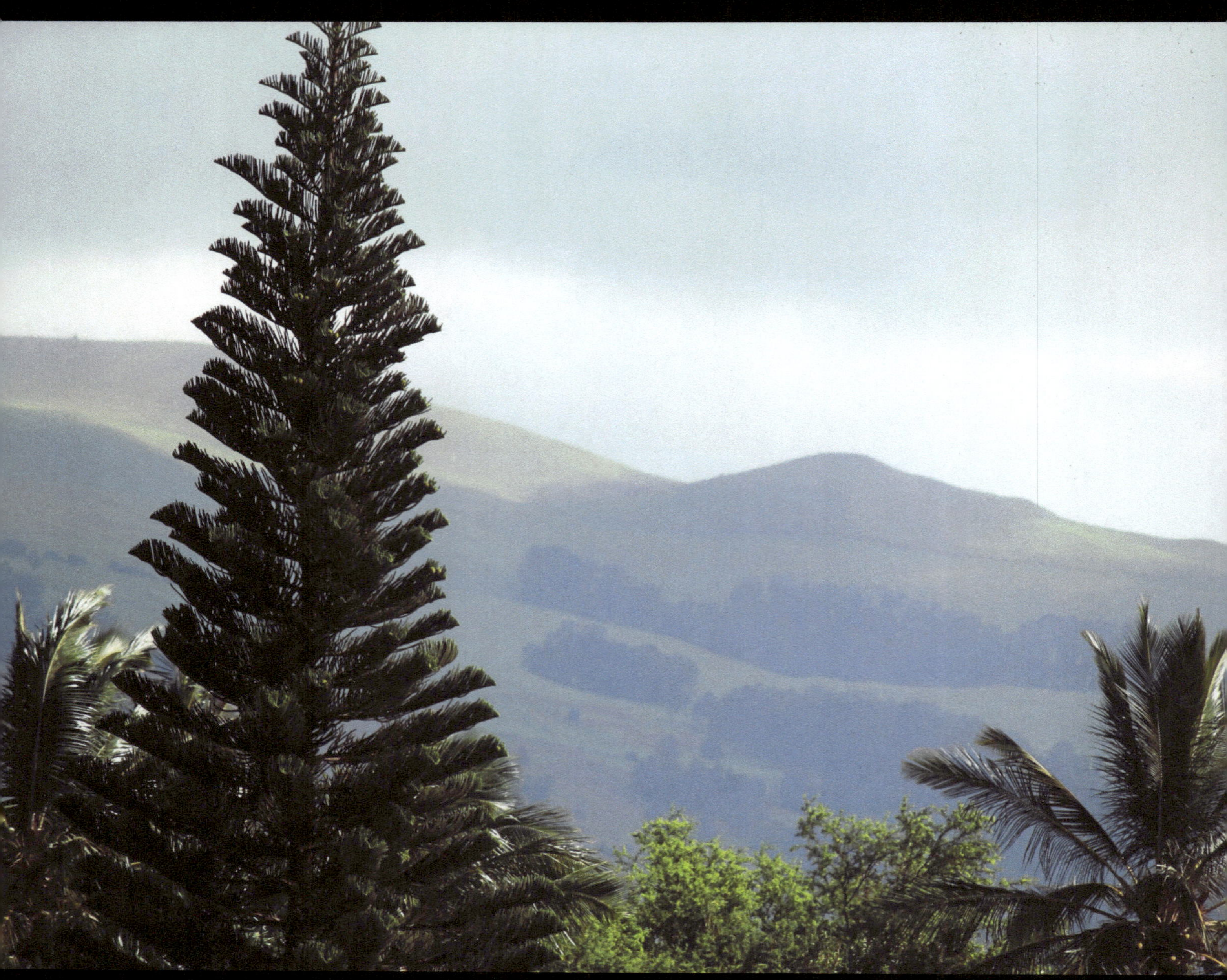

Kihei - Maui, Hawai'i

Psalms 37:1-9

Forgive, be patient, and be angry no more.

The Divine will grant your heart's desire.

"Do not strive to out do the evildoers or emulate those who do wrong. For like the grass, they soon wither and fade like the green of spring. Trust in the LORD and do good... Depend upon the LORD, and He will grant you your heart's desire. Commit your life to the LORD; trust in Him and He will bring it to pass. He will make your righteousness shine forth as the light, and the right of your cause, like the sun at noonday. Wait quietly for the LORD, be patient until He comes... Be angry no more, and put away your vengeance; and do not worry - it only causes harm... For evildoers will be destroyed; but those that wait on the LORD, they shall inherit the earth."

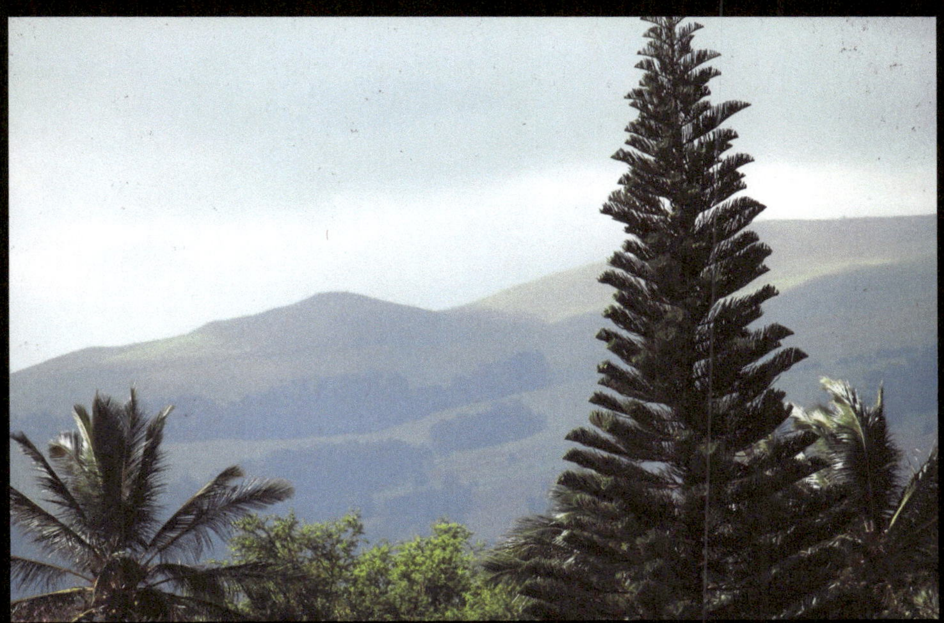

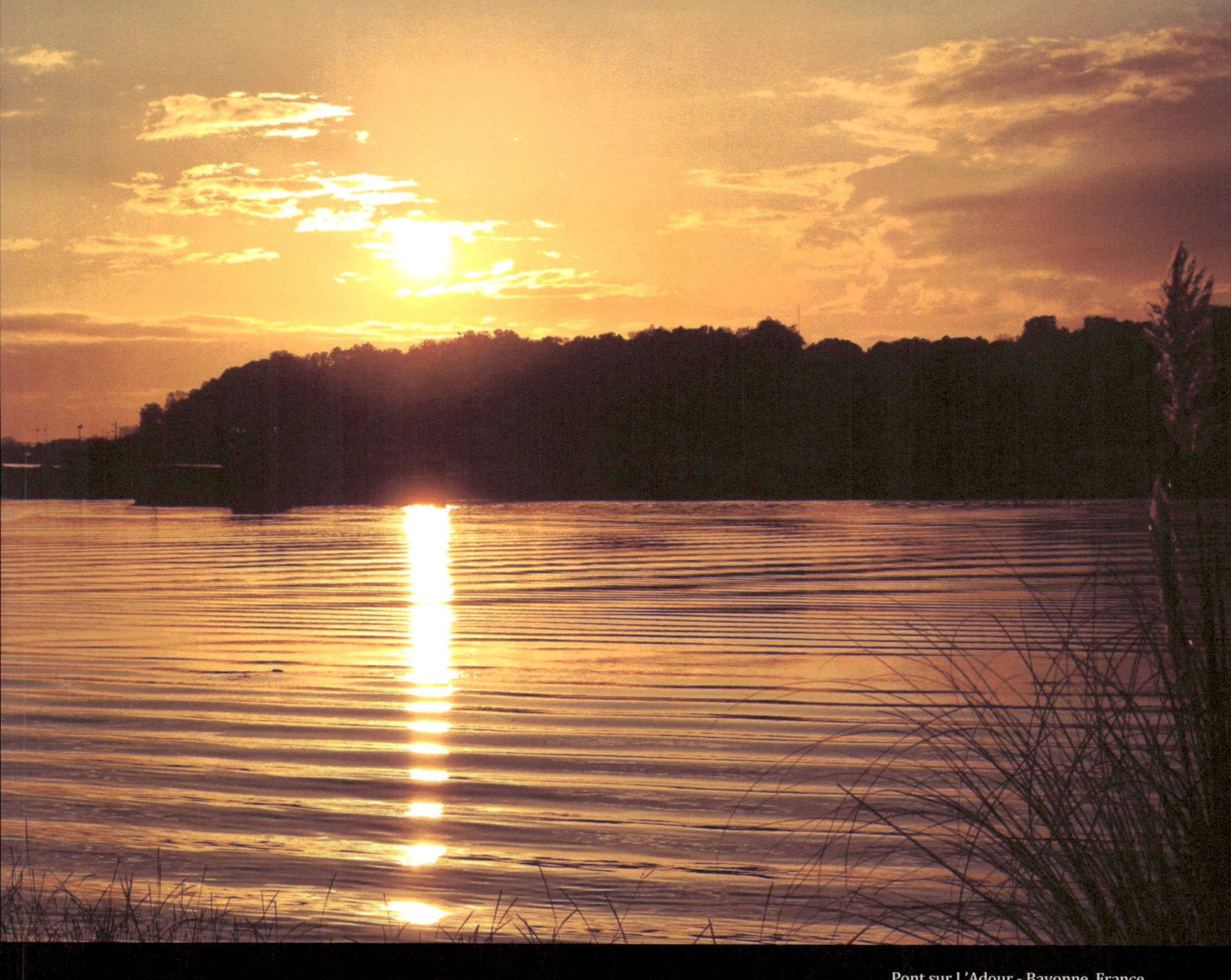

Pont sur L'Adour - Bayonne, France

Isaiah 43:19

Begin something new.

What you can perceive can be achieved. Lay your plans.

"Here and now I do a new thing; this moment it will spring forth. Can you not perceive it? I will even make a way through the wilderness, and rivers in the barren desert..."

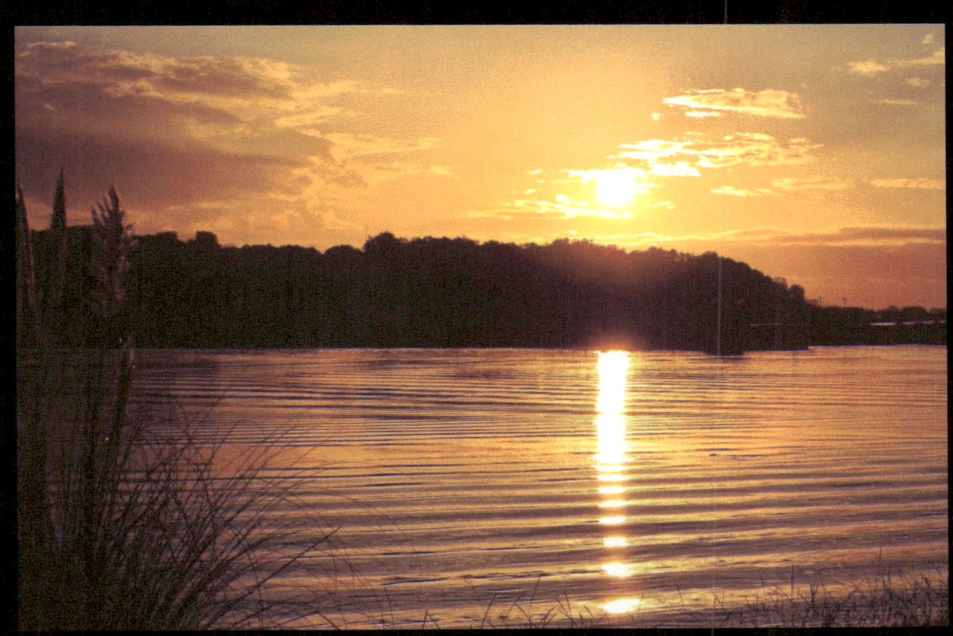

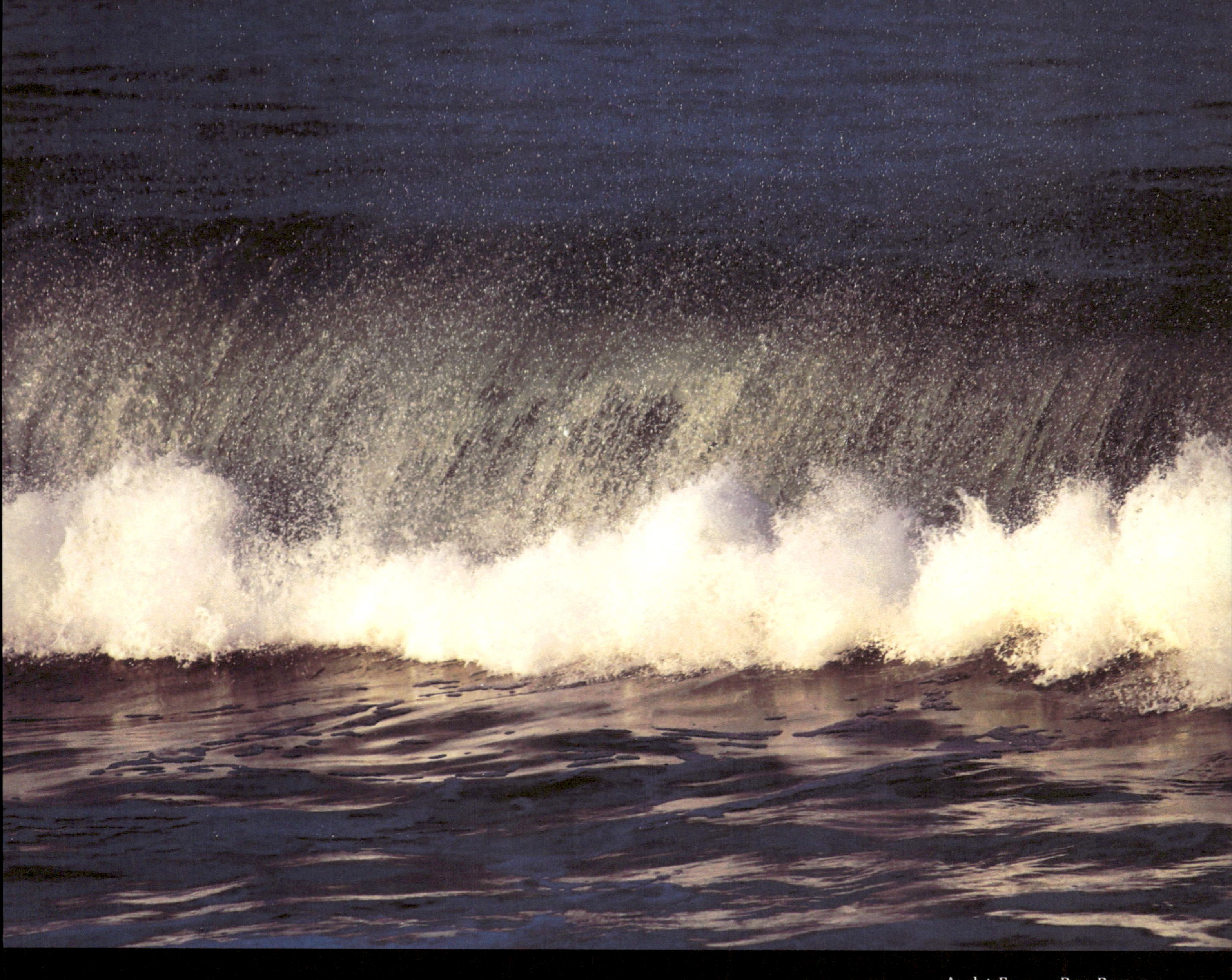
Anglet, France - Pays Basque

Persevere in your struggles and always have hope.

"Therefore, since we have been justified through faith, we have peace with The Divine GOD through our Lord, Yeshua, Jesus Christ; through whom we have gained access by faith into this grace in which we stand. And we rejoice in the hope of the glory of GOD. And so, we also rejoice in our suffering, because we know that suffering produces perseverance; perseverance character, and character – hope. And hope does not disappoint us, because the love of GOD has been poured out into our hearts by the Holy Spirit."

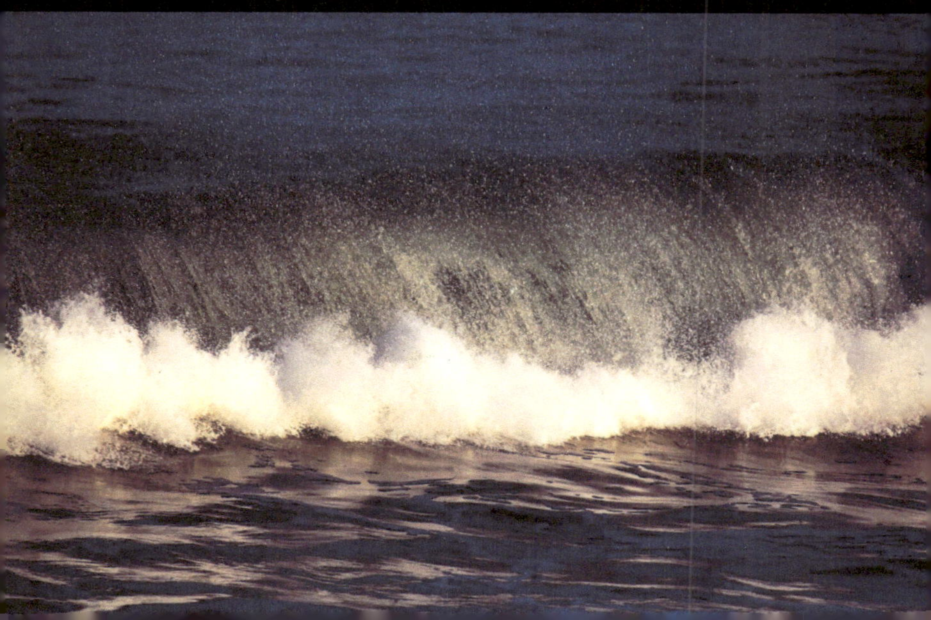

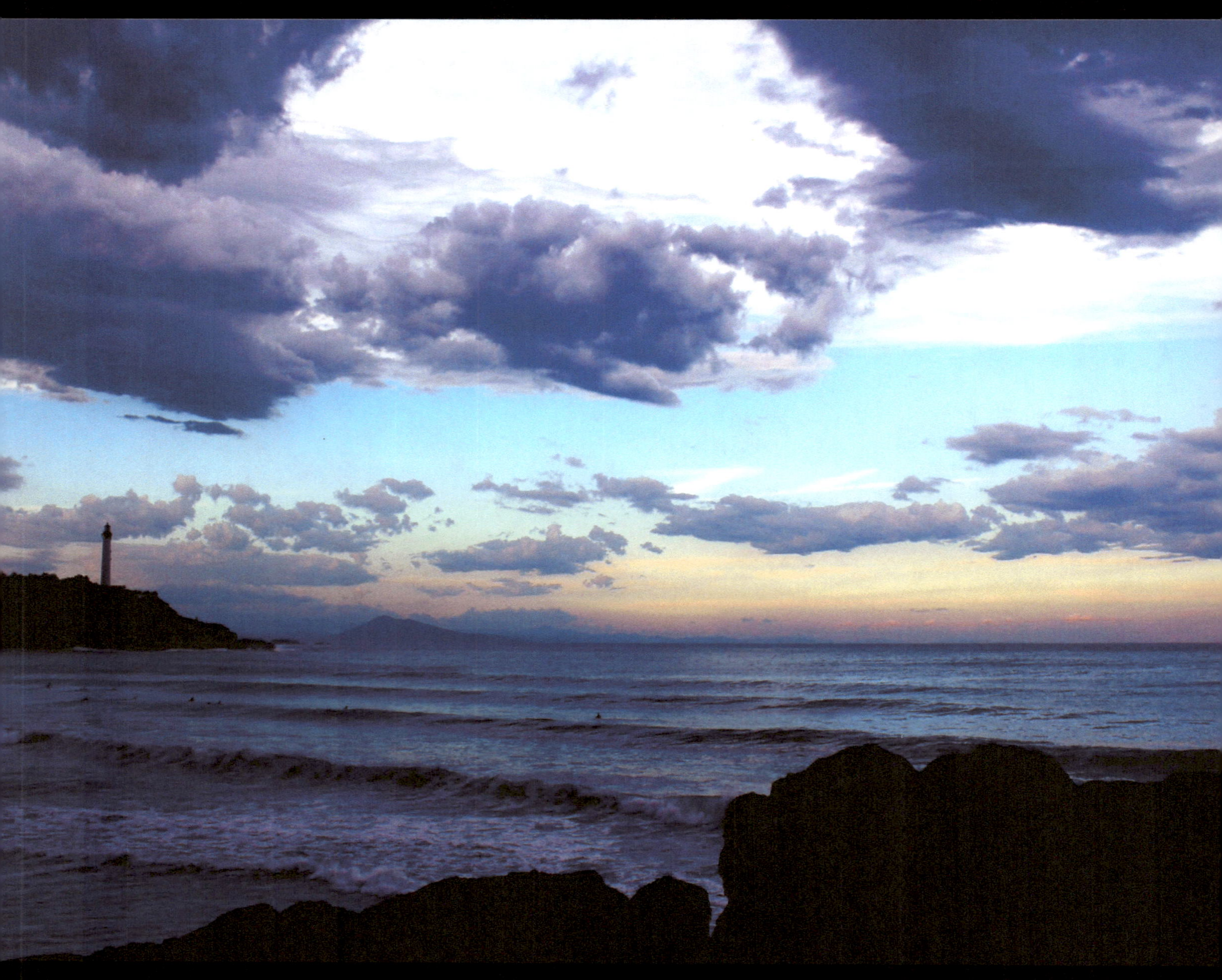

Pays Basque - Anglet, France

Mathew 21:21-22

With faith you can move mountains.

"I tell you this: If only you have faith and no doubts, you will do what has been done to the fig tree and more than that. The fig tree was cursed by Jesus because it did not bear any fruit and he and the disciples were hungry. The fig tree immediately withered.) You need only say to the mountain, 'Be lifted from your place and hurled into the sea', and what you say will be done. And whatever you pray for, believing, you will receive."

(Jesus Christ)

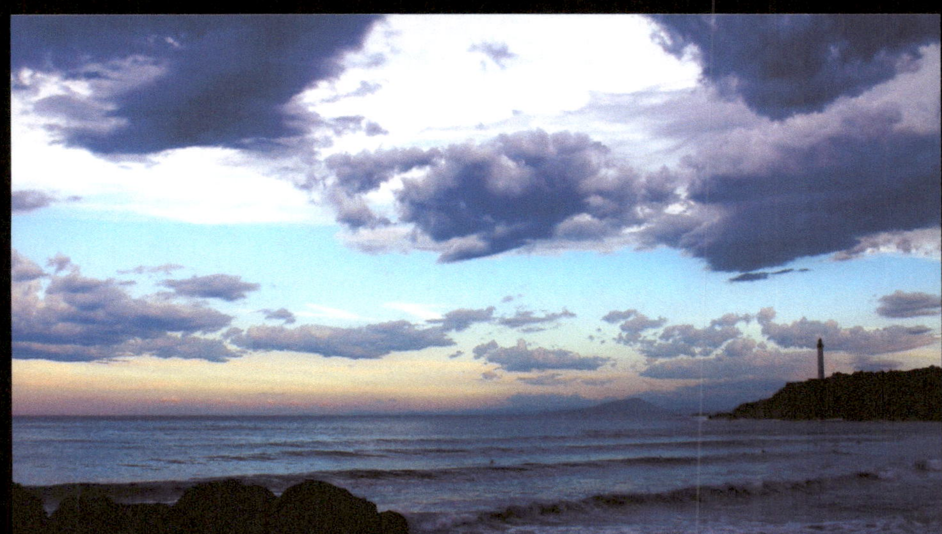

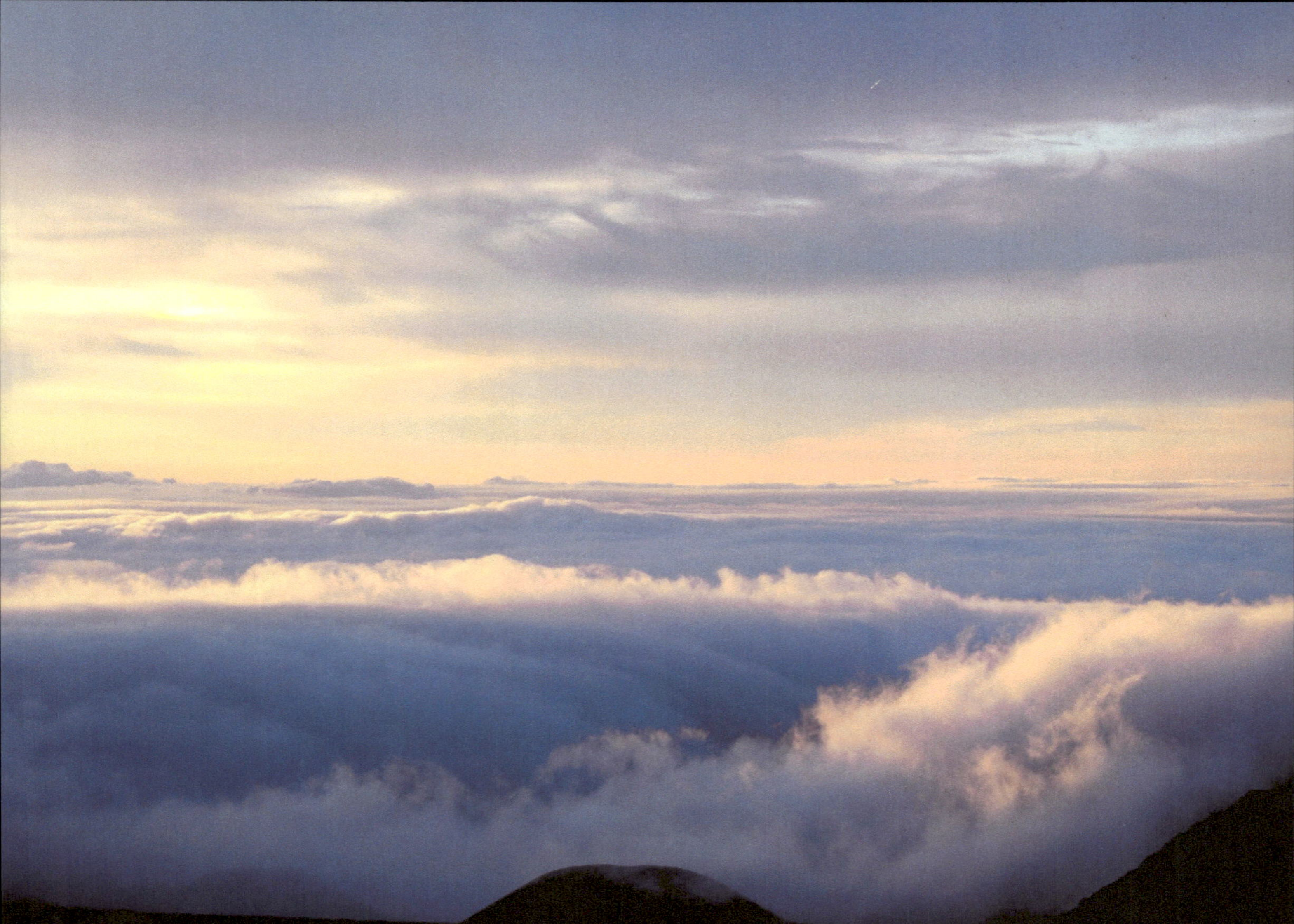

Isaiah 40:28-41

The Divine gives you strength and courage.

"The LORD, the everlasting GOD, creator of the wide world, grows neither weary nor faint. No man can fathom his understanding. He gives power to the weak, and to those who are exhausted, He gives strength. Even the young will get tired and become weary, and the young men shall truly fall; but they that wait on the LORD shall renew their strength, they shall mount up with wings as eagles, they shall run and not be weary; they shall walk and not faint."

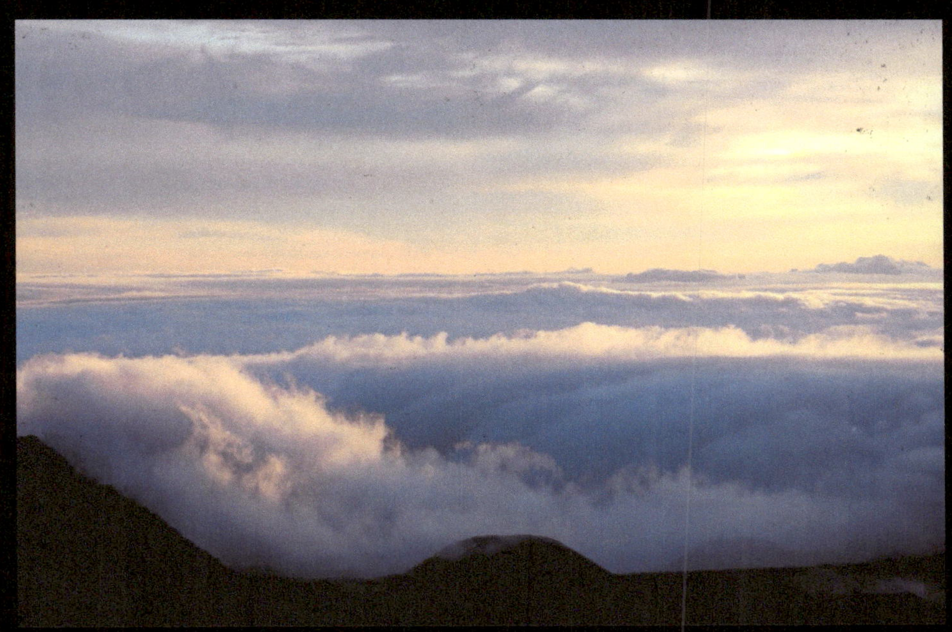

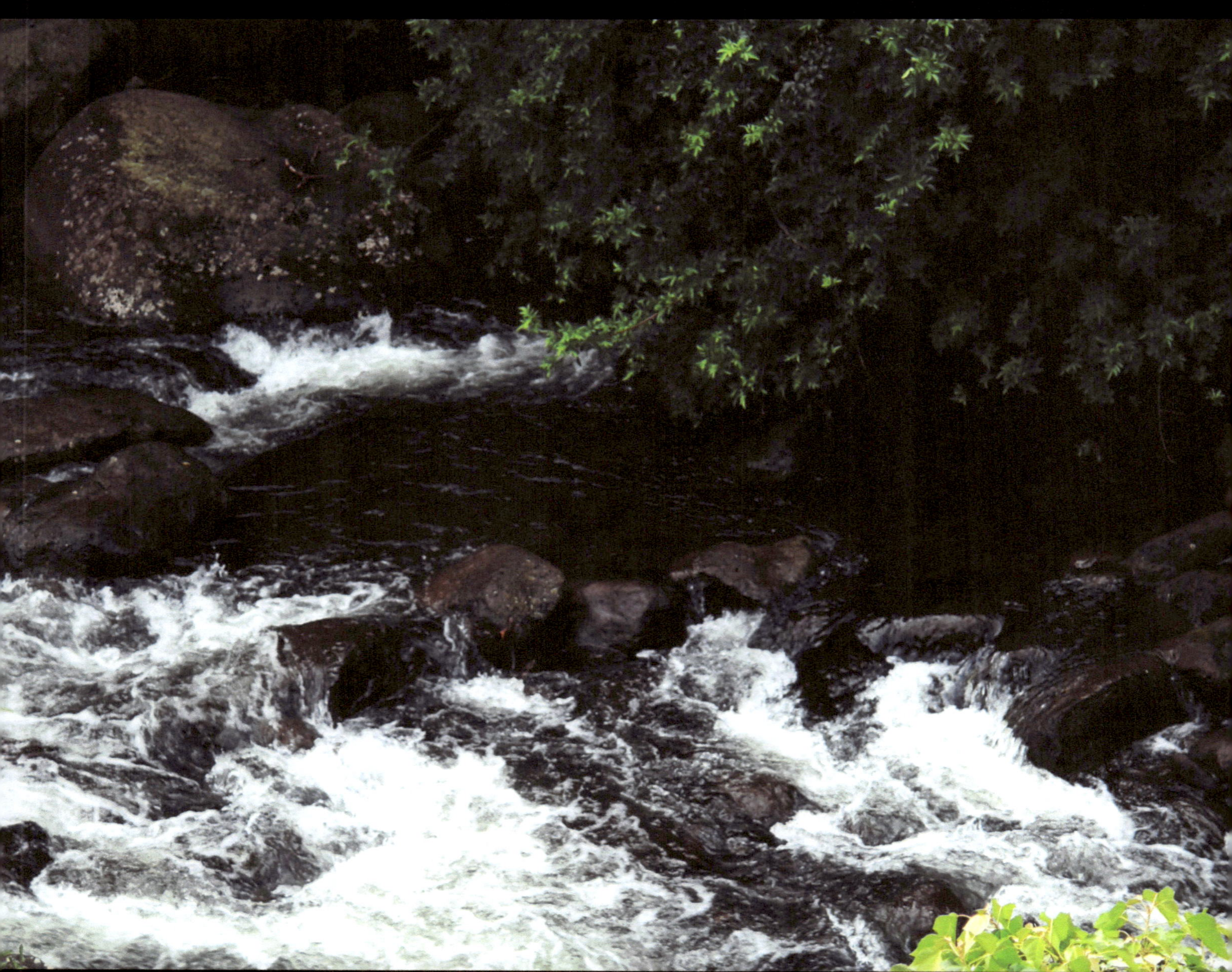

Iao Valley - Maui, Hawai'i

John 14:13-14

Your prayers will be granted.

"Whatever you shall ask in My name that I will do, so that the Father may be glorified in the Son. If you ask anything in my name I will do it."
(Jesus Christ)

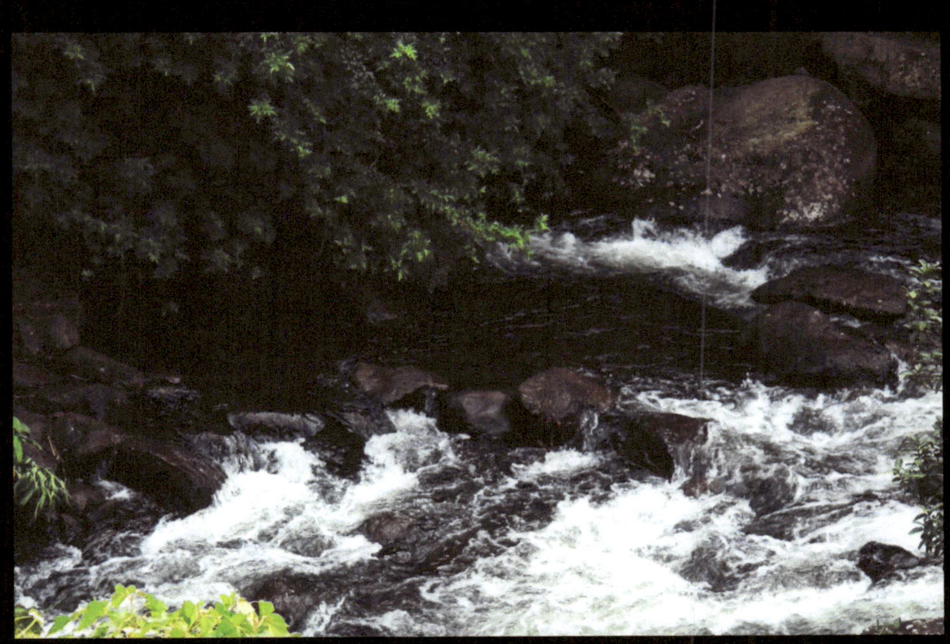

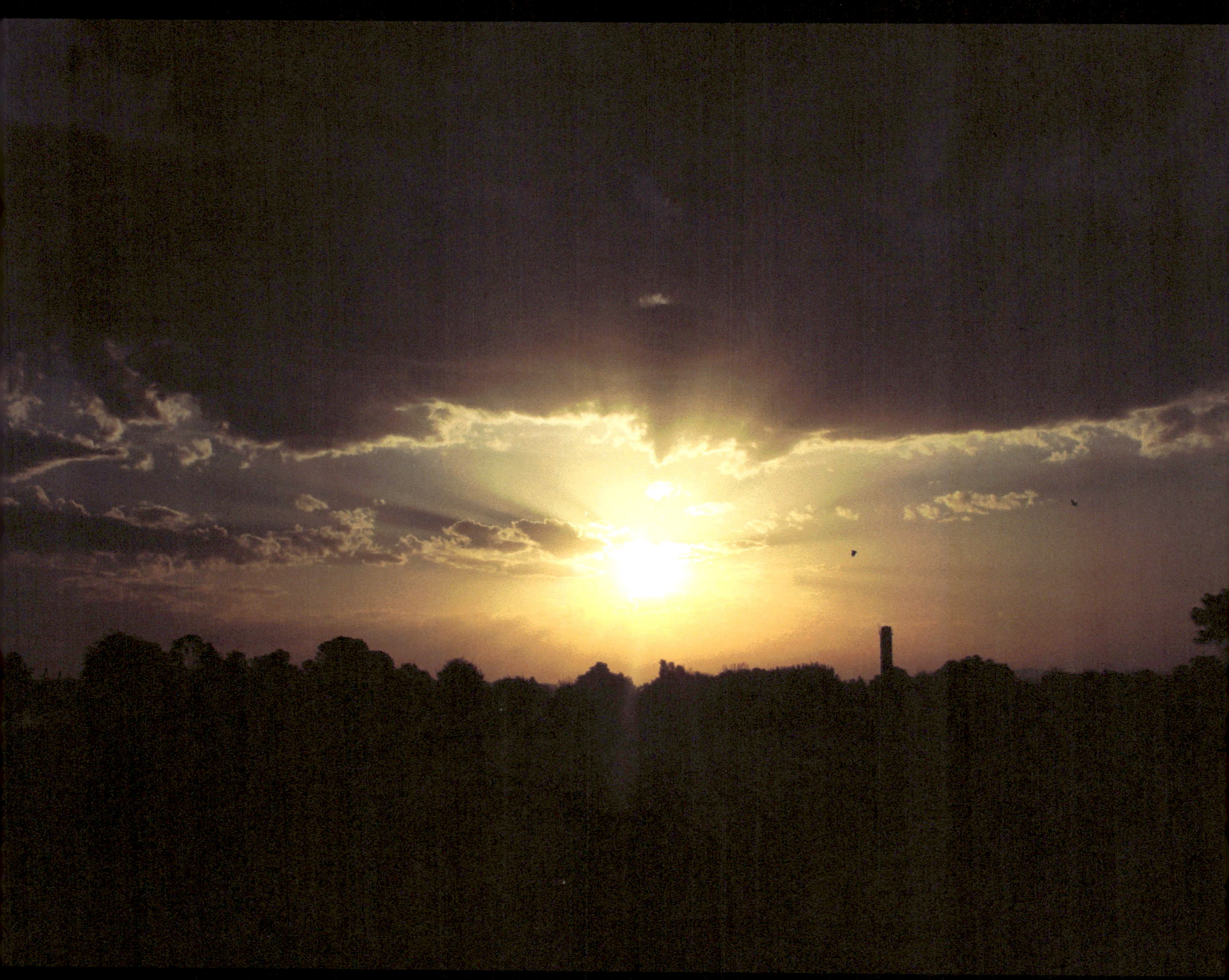

Sunrise Cinq Cantons - Anglet, France

Hebrews 11:1, 6

Faith is the substance of things hoped for,
and the evidence of things unseen.

"Without Faith it is impossible to please GOD, for he who comes to The LORD must believe that He is, and that He rewards those who diligently seek Him."

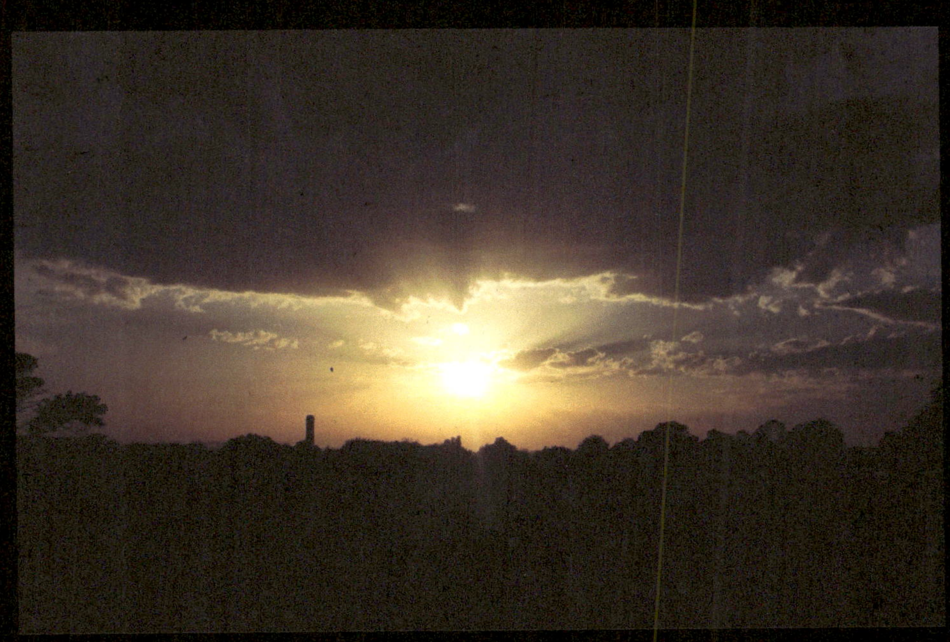

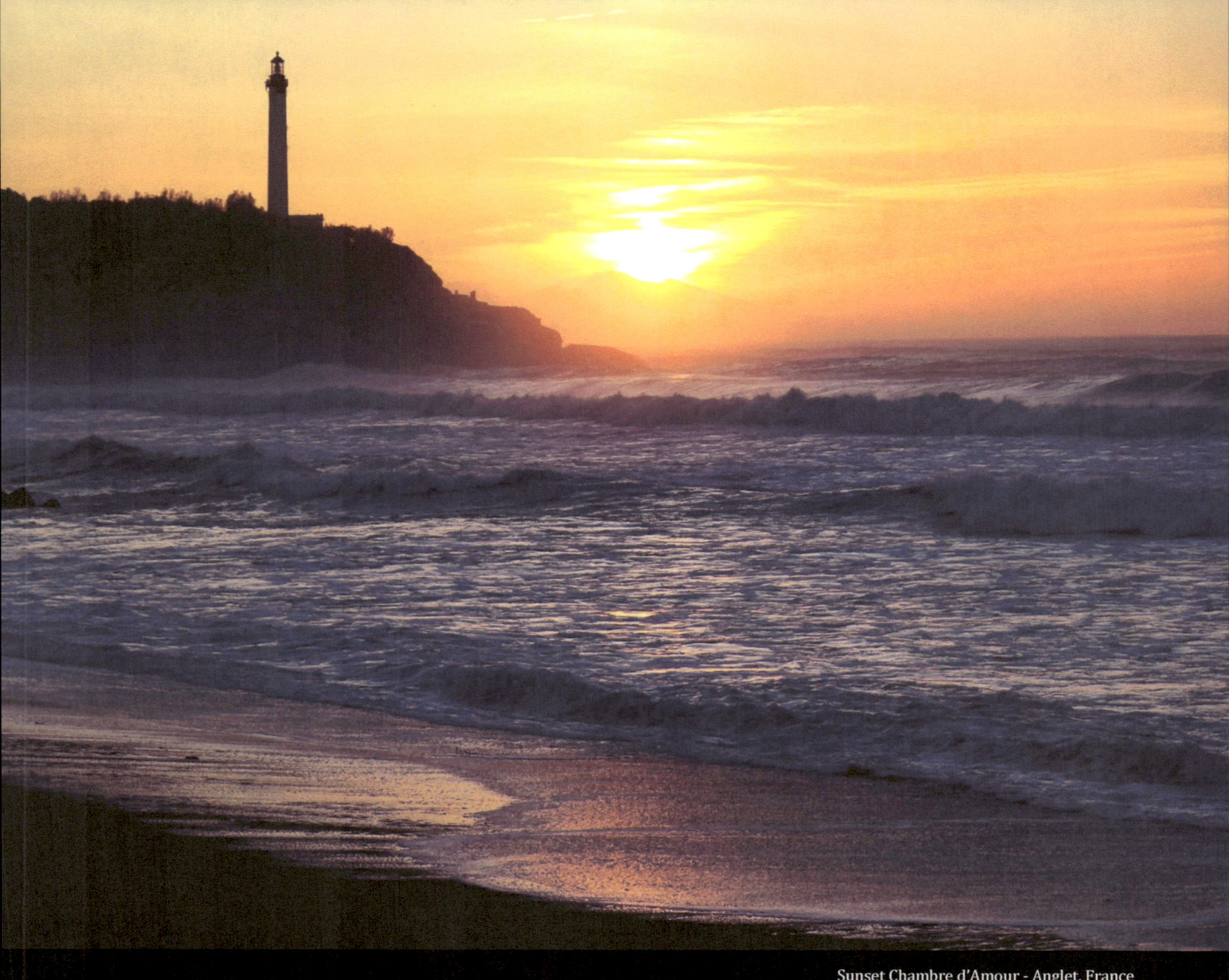

Sunset Chambre d'Amour - Anglet, France

Mathew 11:28-30

Rest from your worries.

Trust in GOD and you will be at peace.

"Come to me, all of you who labor and are very tired, and I will give you rest. Take what I have to offer and learn from me; for I am gentle and humble in my heart, and you will find rest within your souls. For what I require of you is easy and my burden is light."

(Jesus Christ)

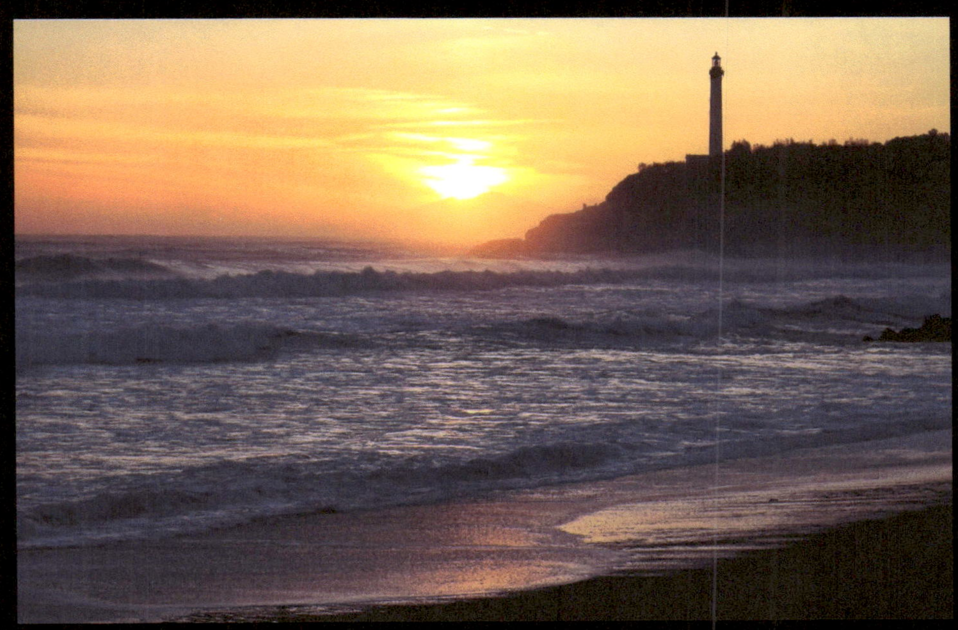

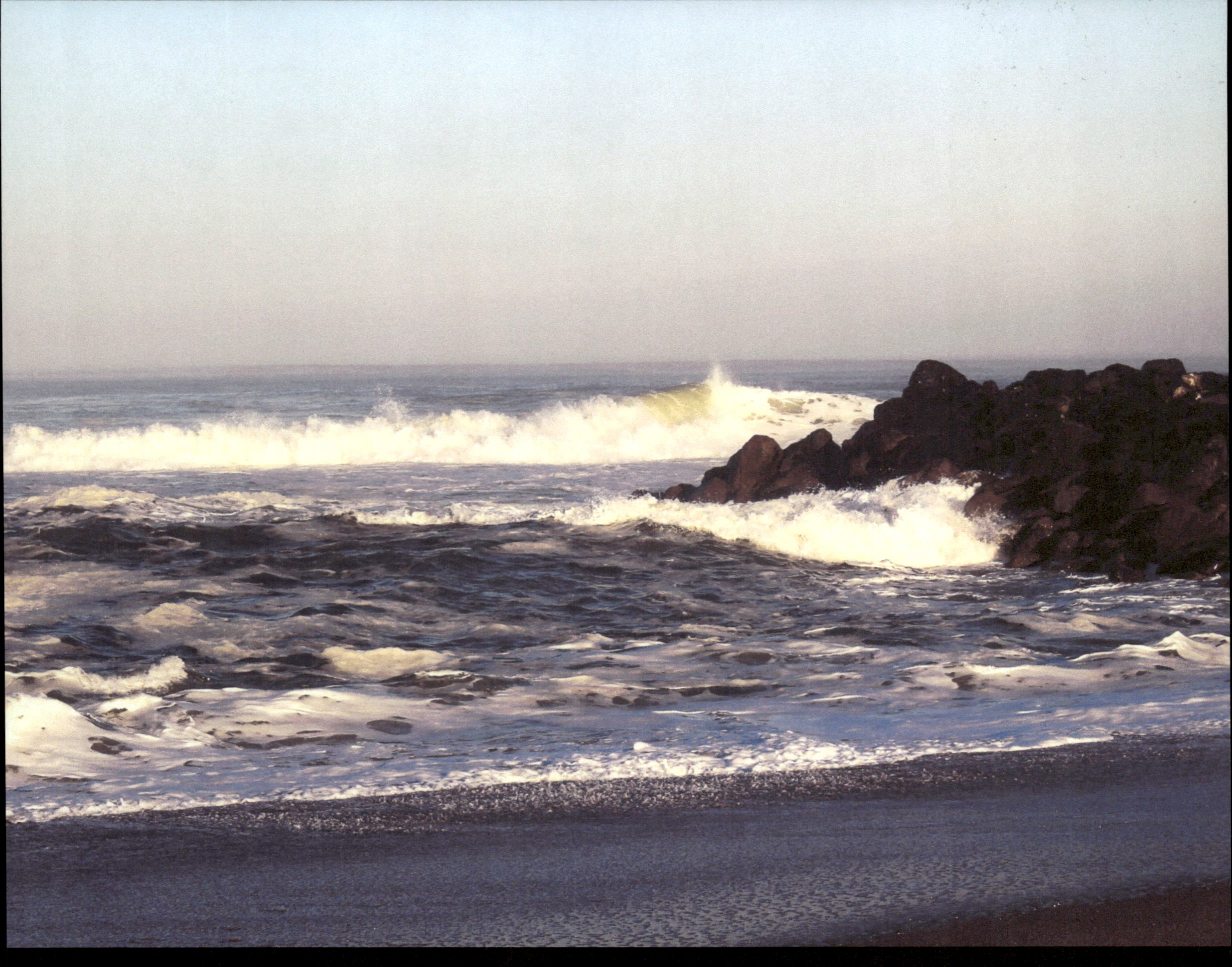

Pay Basque - Aquitaine, France

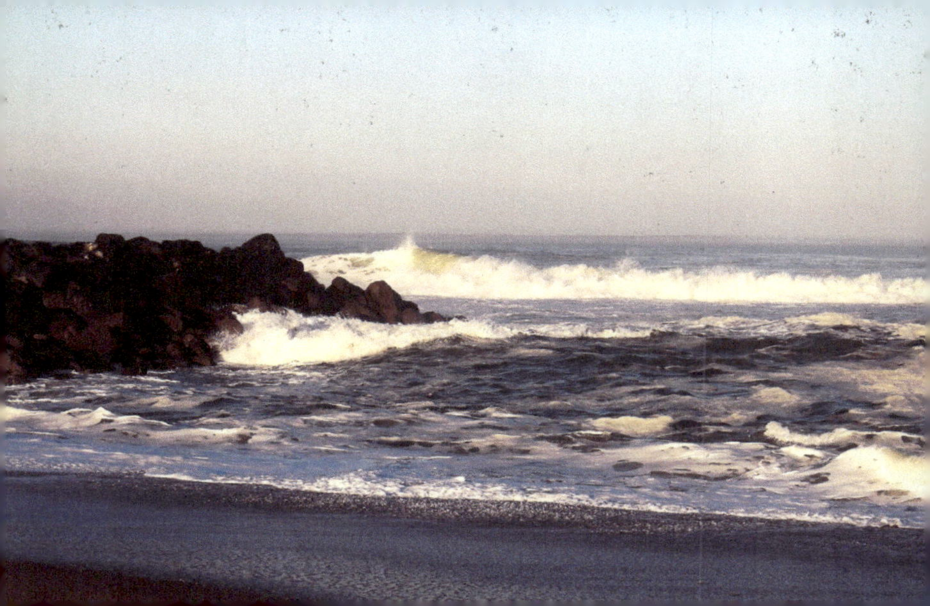

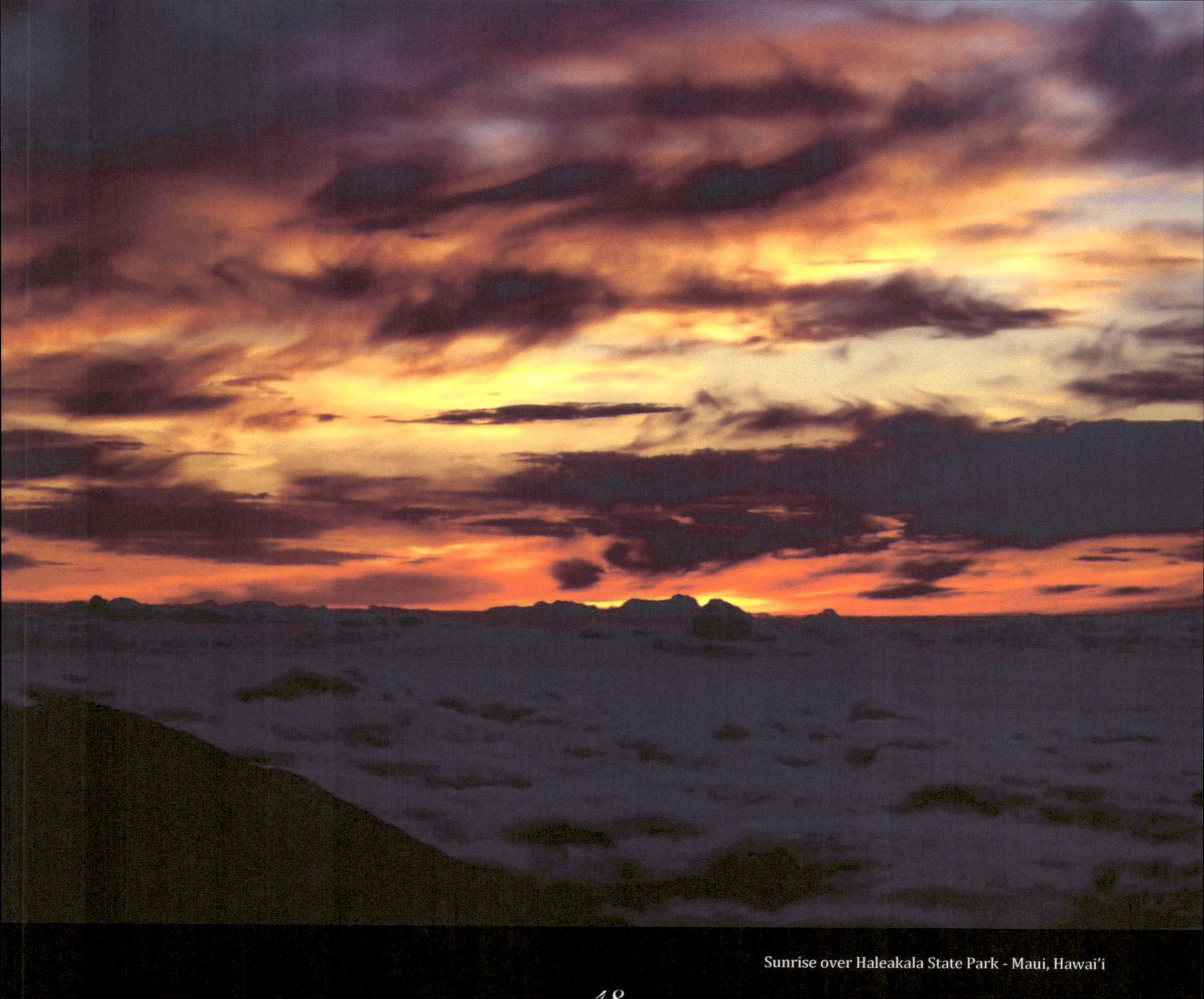

Sunrise over Haleakala State Park - Maui, Hawai'i

Mathew 9:20-22

Your faith will heal you.

"...Then a woman who suffered from hemorrhages for twelve years came from behind, and touched the hem of his garment; for she said to herself, 'If I can only touch his cloak, I shall be healed.' But Yeshua (Jesus) turned and when he saw her, he said, 'Take heart, my daughter; your faith has made you whole.' And the woman was healed from that hour."

(Jesus Christ)

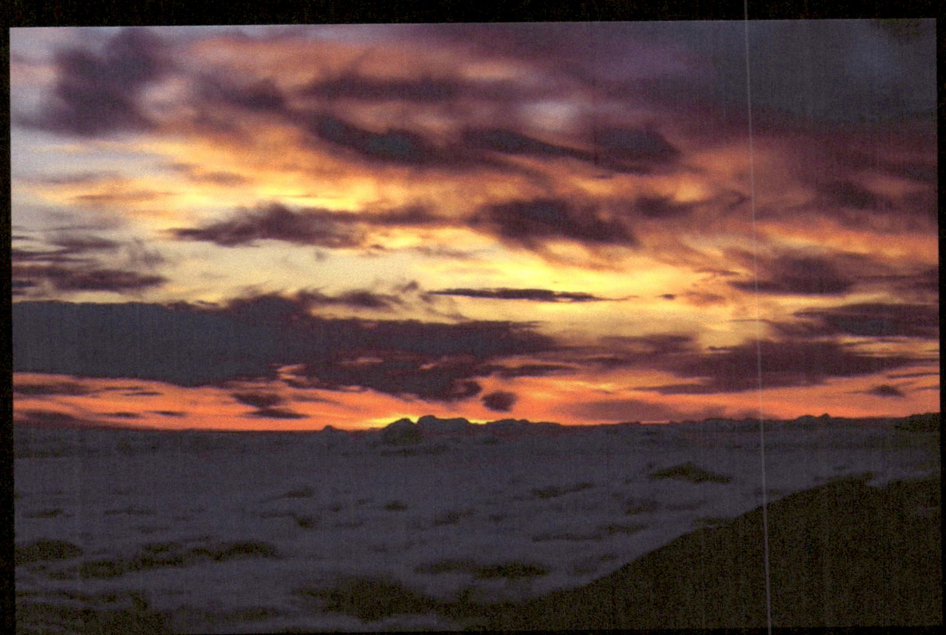

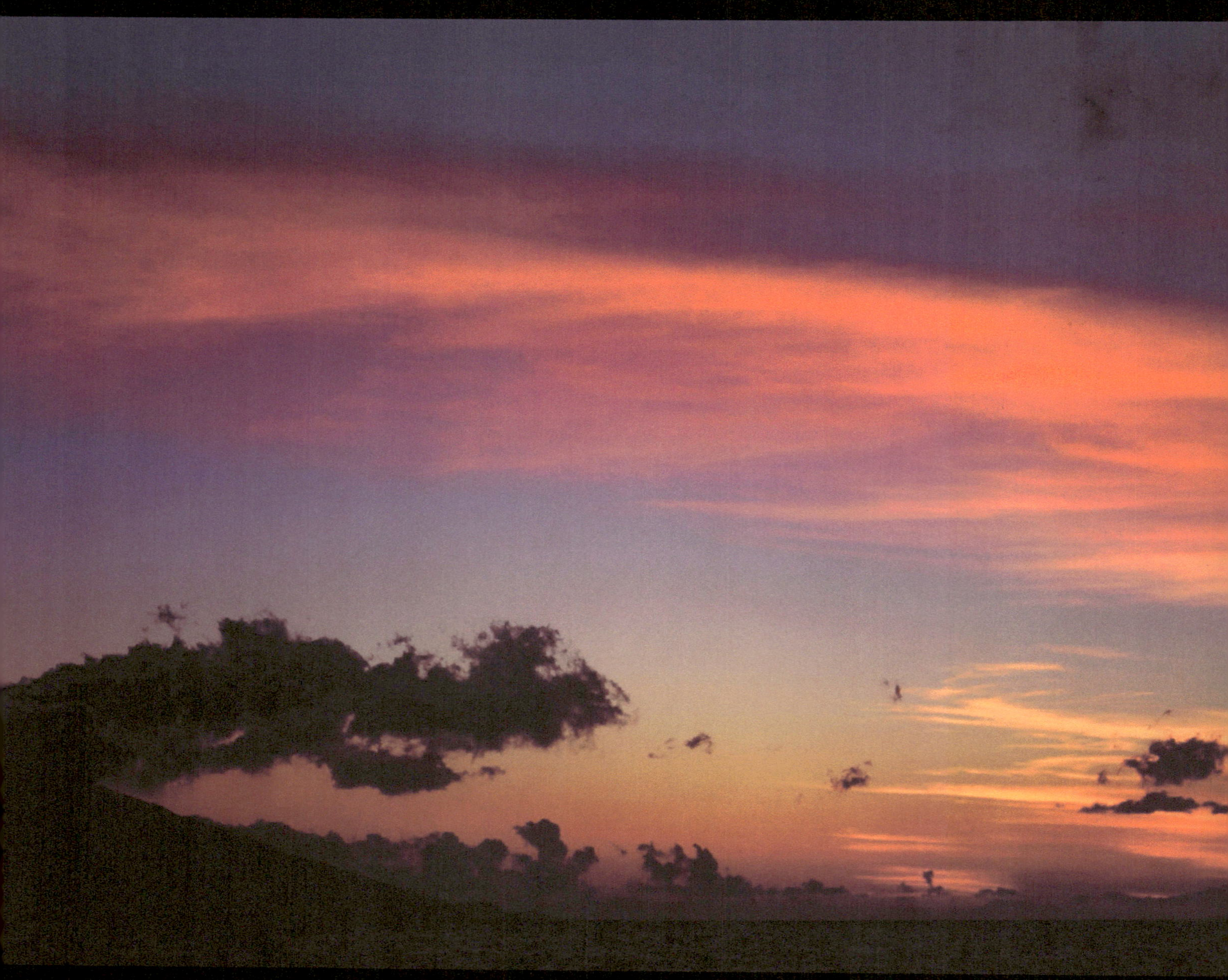

Sunset Kihei - Maui, Hawai'i

Jonah 2:2-5, 7

Praise GOD through your troubles and He will deliver you.
The Divine is a GOD of second chances.

"And Jonah prayed to the LORD from inside the belly of the fish, 'and he said: I cried out to the LORD in my sufferings and He heard me. I begged you from the pit of hell and you heard my voice. For I am thrown down into the depths of the sea and the currents swirled all around me and the whirlpools and waves passed over me... The waters surrounded me, even to my soul. The abyss has trapped me and I was drowning, the ocean was covering my head. But when my life with nearly gone, I remembered you and in heaven you heard my prayer."

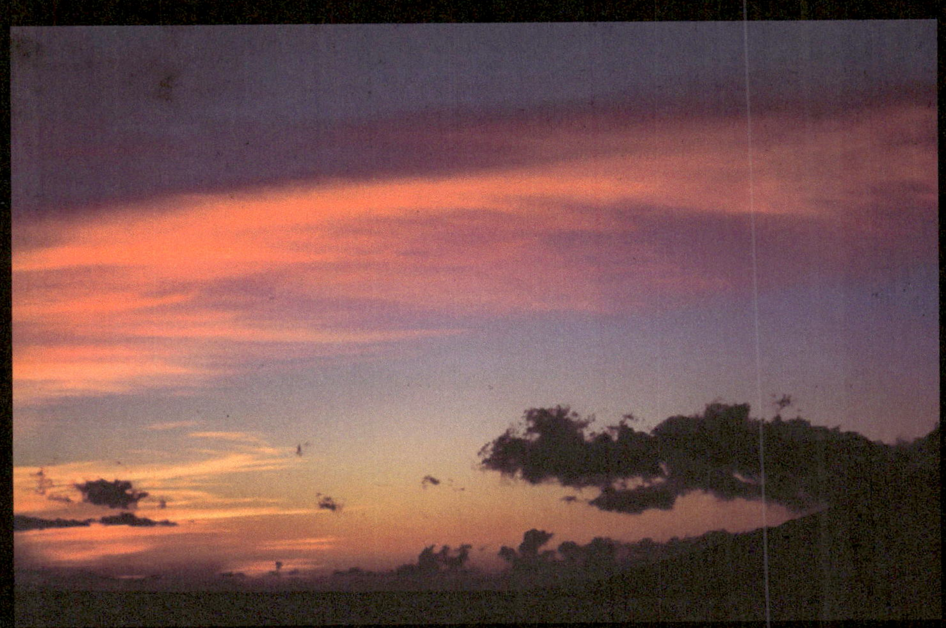

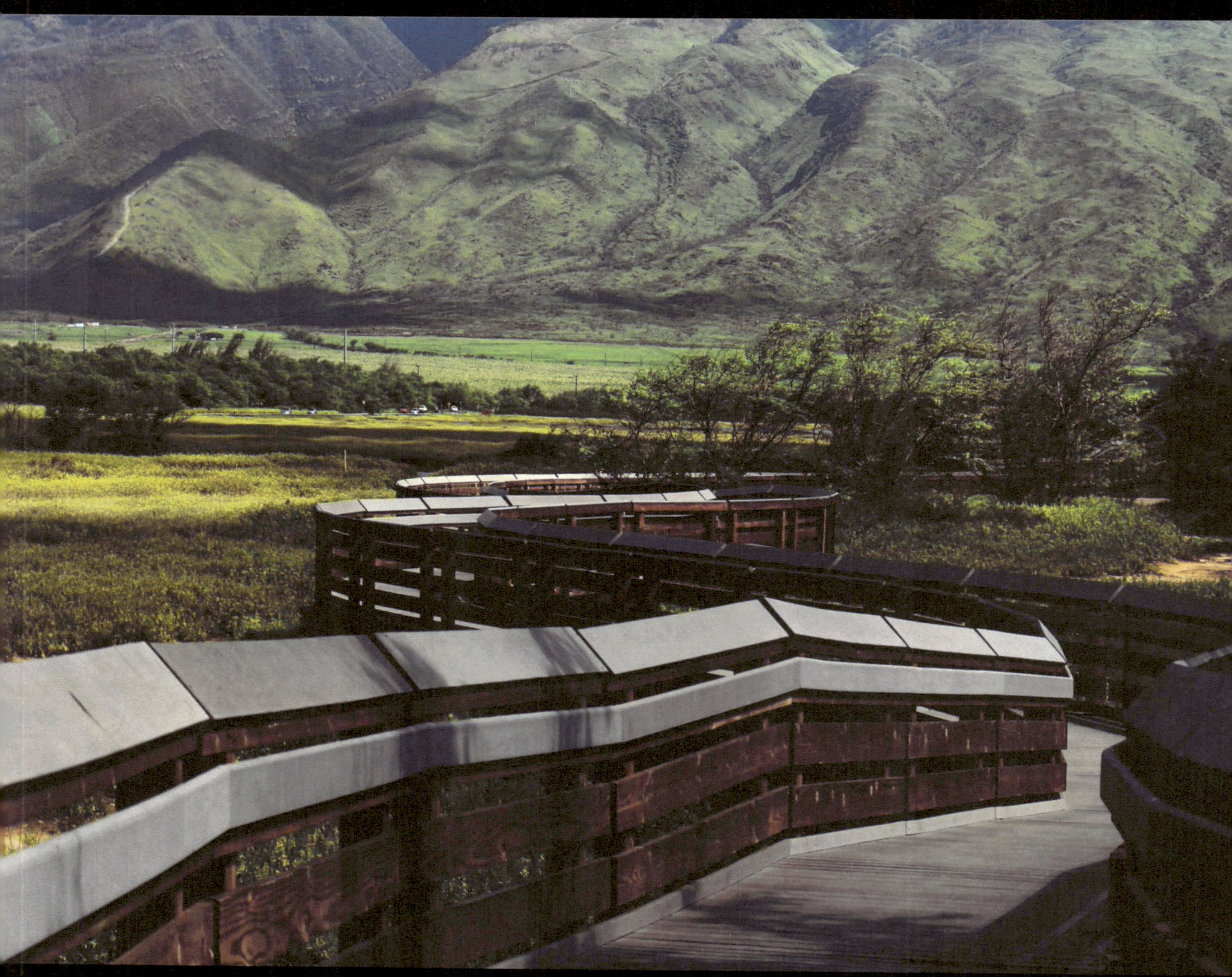

Island of Maui, Hawai'i

Mathew 17:20-21

Faith, prayer, and fasting, makes the impossible, possible.

"Your faith is too small. I tell you this: If you have faith no bigger than a mustard seed, you can say to this mountain, 'Move from here to there!', and it will move. Nothing will prove impossible for you. However, this can only be manifested by prayer and fasting."

(Jesus Christ)

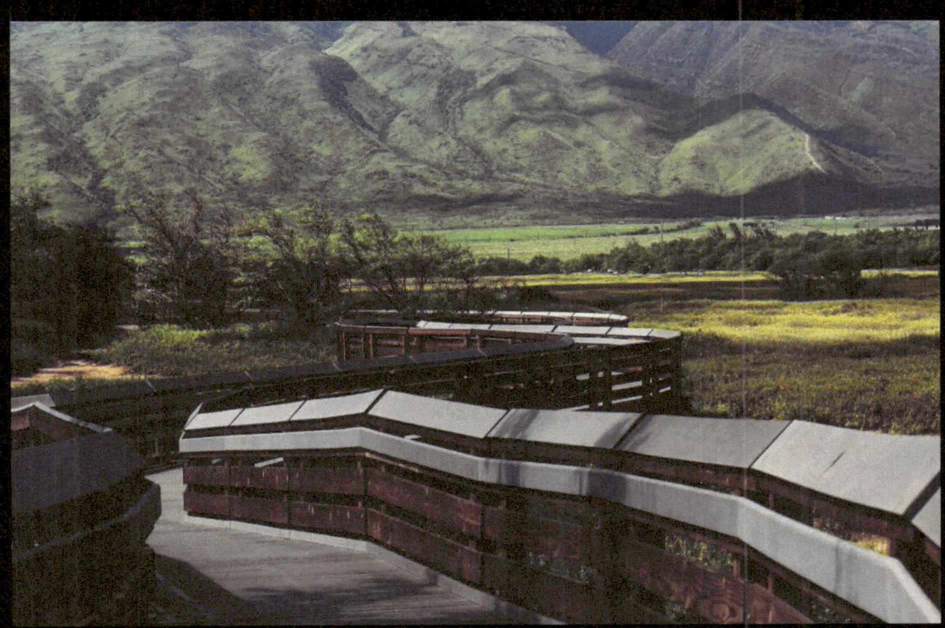

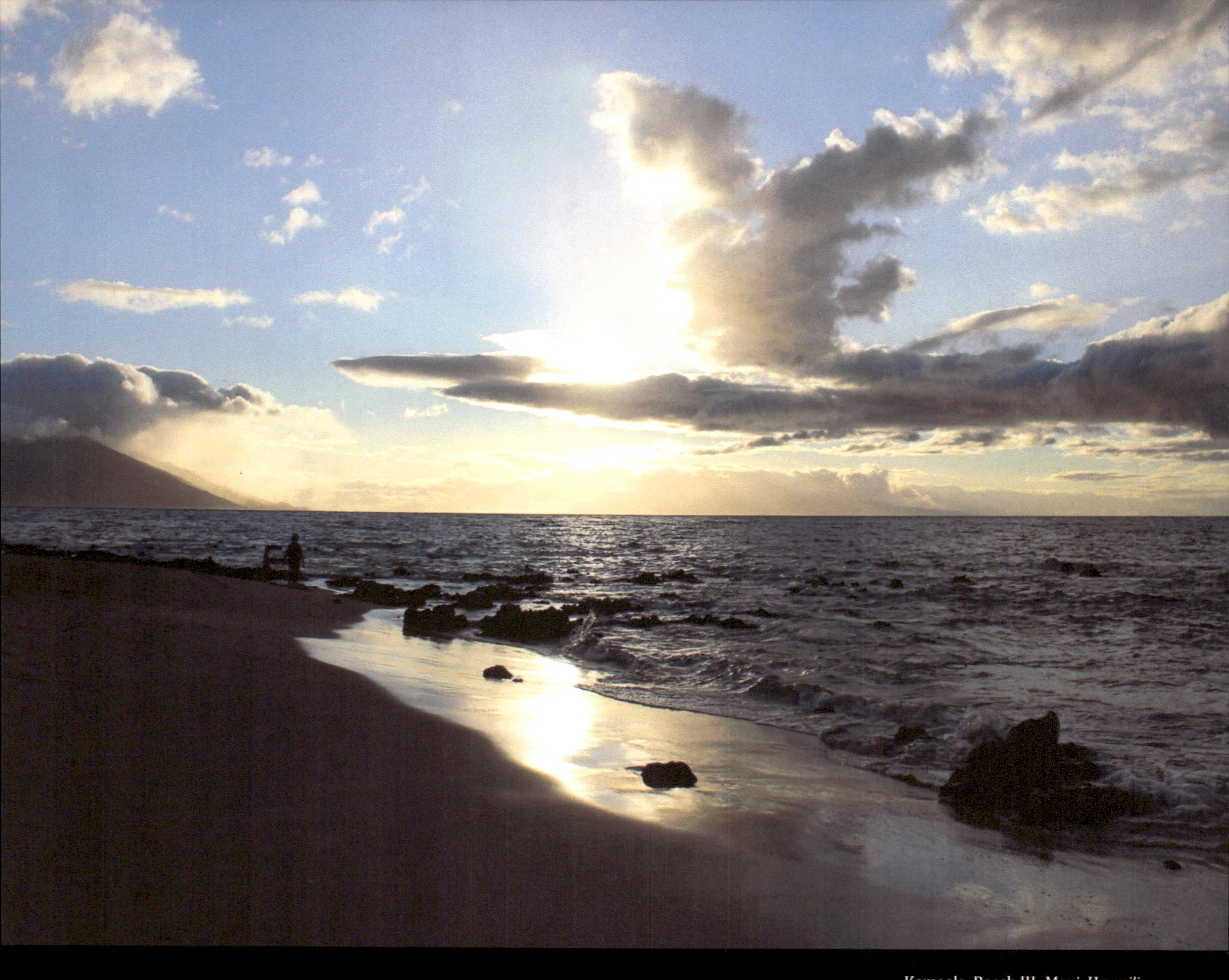

Kamaole Beach III- Maui, Hawai'i

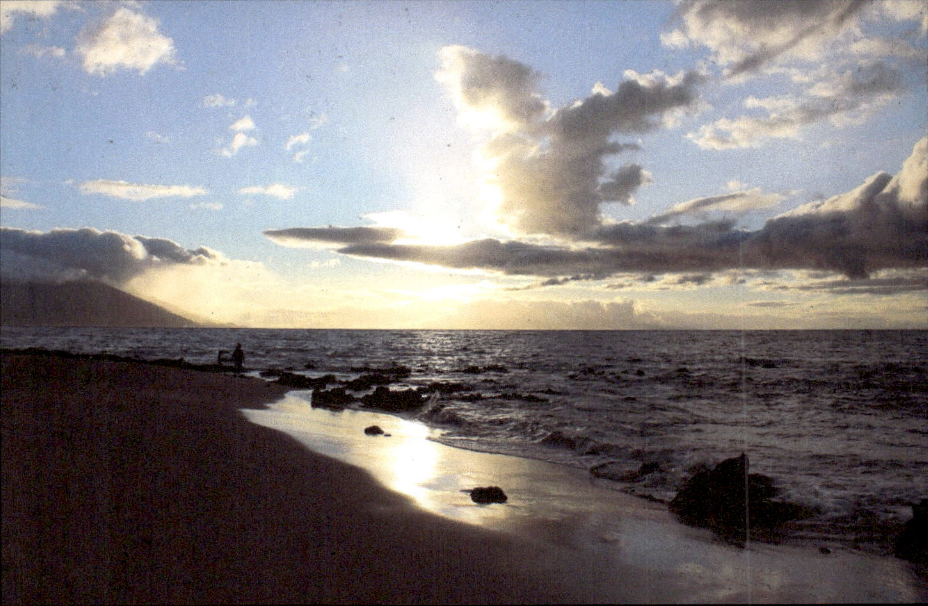

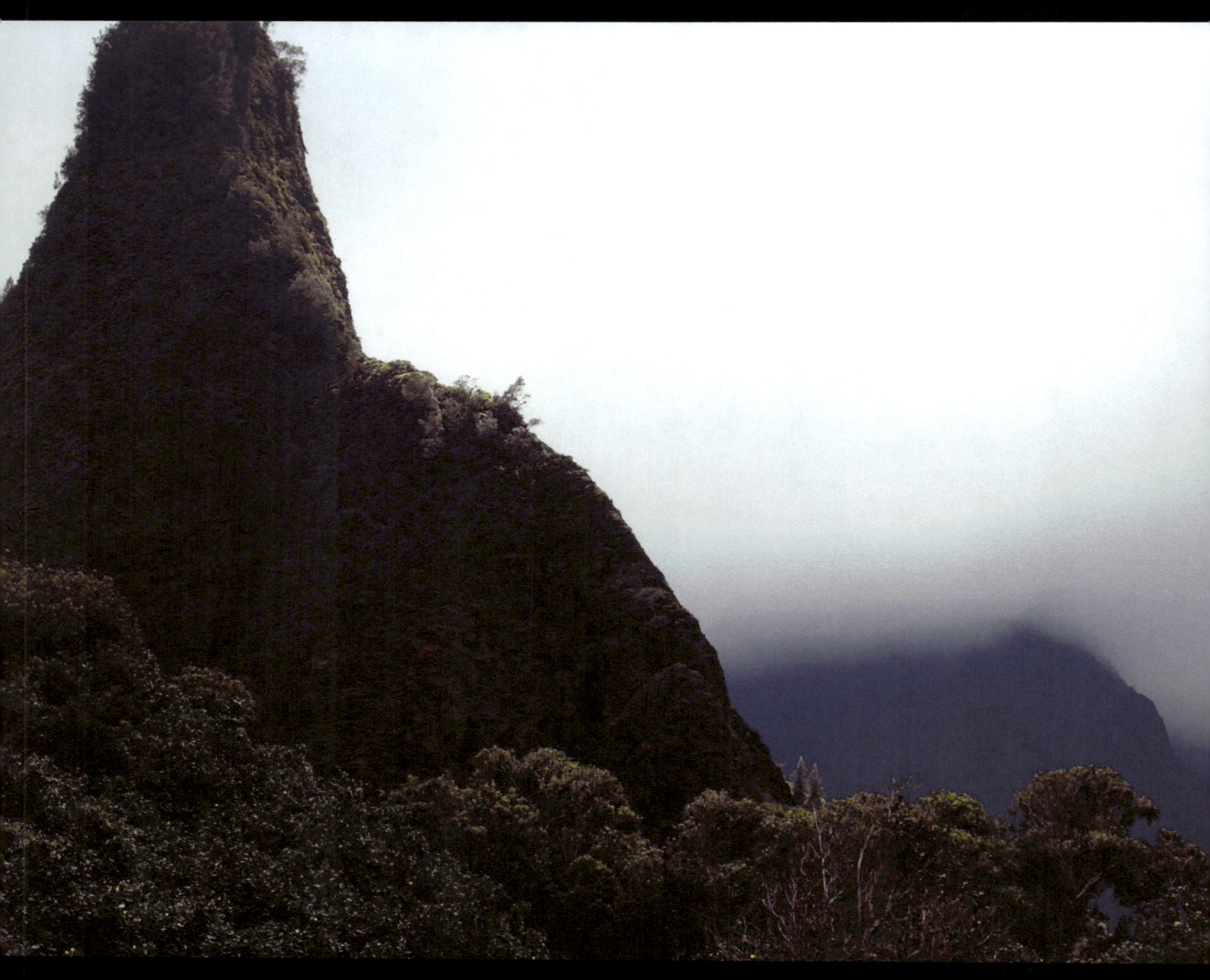

Iao Valley - Maui, Hawai'i

Romans 8:24-25

The Divine will sustain you. Be courageous.

Never be afraid.

"But You, Oh LORD, are a shield for me, My glory, and the One who lifts up my head. I cried to the LORD with my voice, and He heard me from His holy hill. I laid down and slept. I awoke, because the LORD kept me. I will not be afraid of ten thousands men surrounding me."

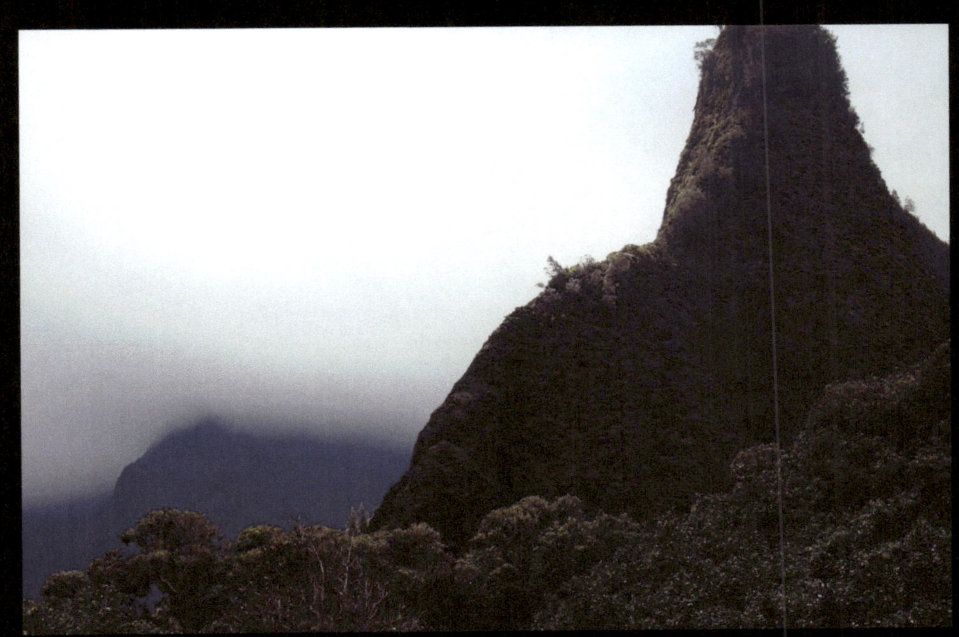

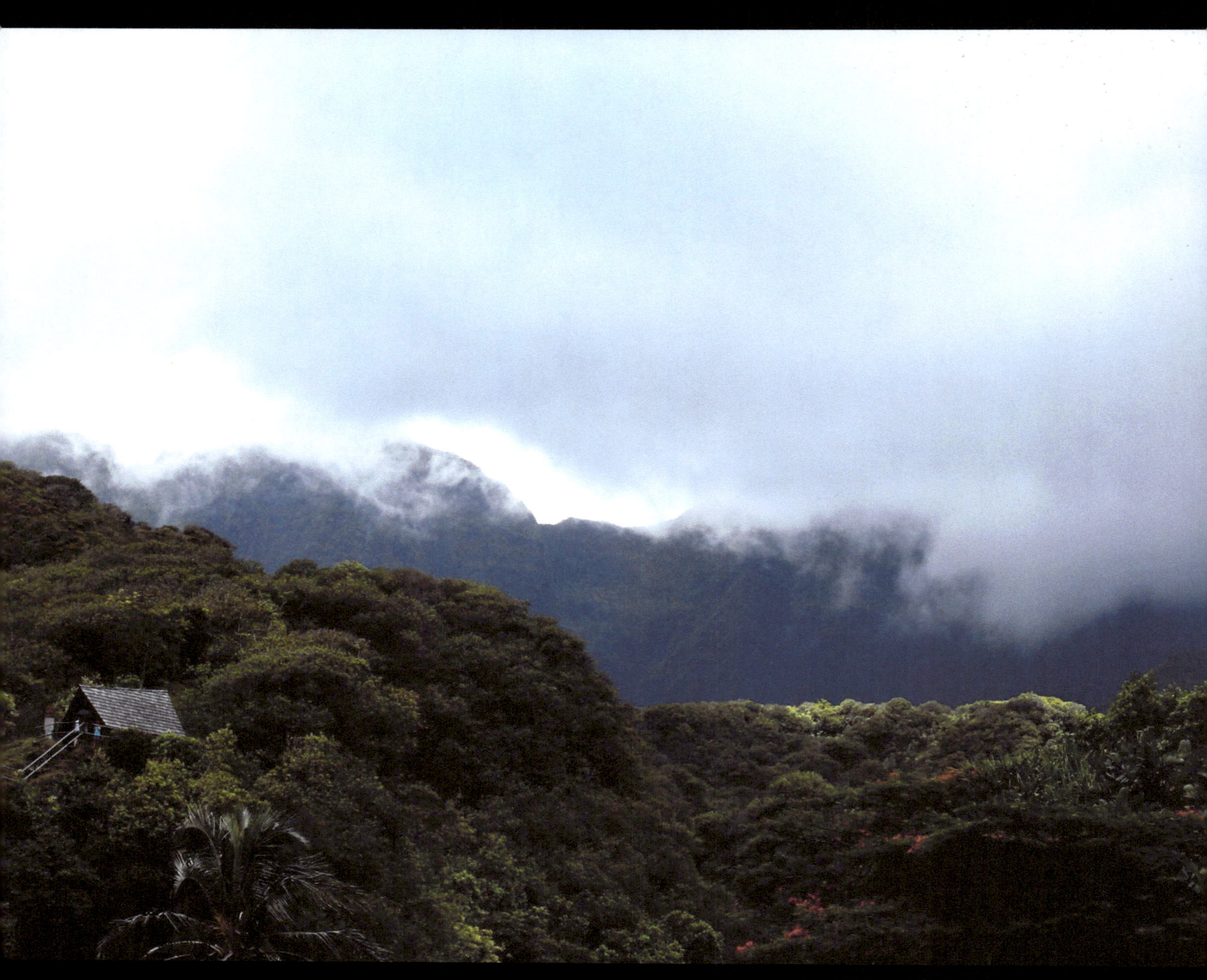

Iao Valley - Maui, Hawai'i

Isaiah 41:13, 17-20

The Divine will help you, the needy, and the poor.

"For I the LORD your GOD will hold your right hand, and say to you, 'Don't be afraid; I will help you'." When the poor and needy search for water and there is none, and they are suffering from thirst, I, The LORD, will hear them. I, The GOD of Israel will not forsake them. I will open rivers in high places and fountains in the midst of the valleys: I will make the wilderness a pool of water, and dry lands springs of water. I will plant in the wilderness the cedar tree... and the myrtle, and the oil tree; I will set in the desert the fir tree, and the pine, and the box tree ensemble: That you may see, and know, reason, and understand together that the hand of The LORD has done this, and that the HOLY ONE... created it."

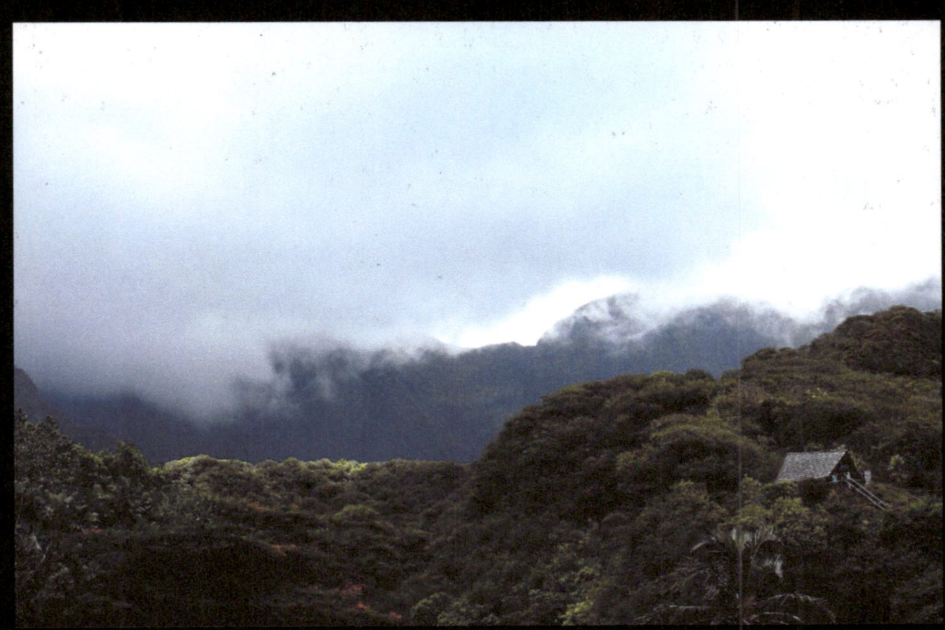

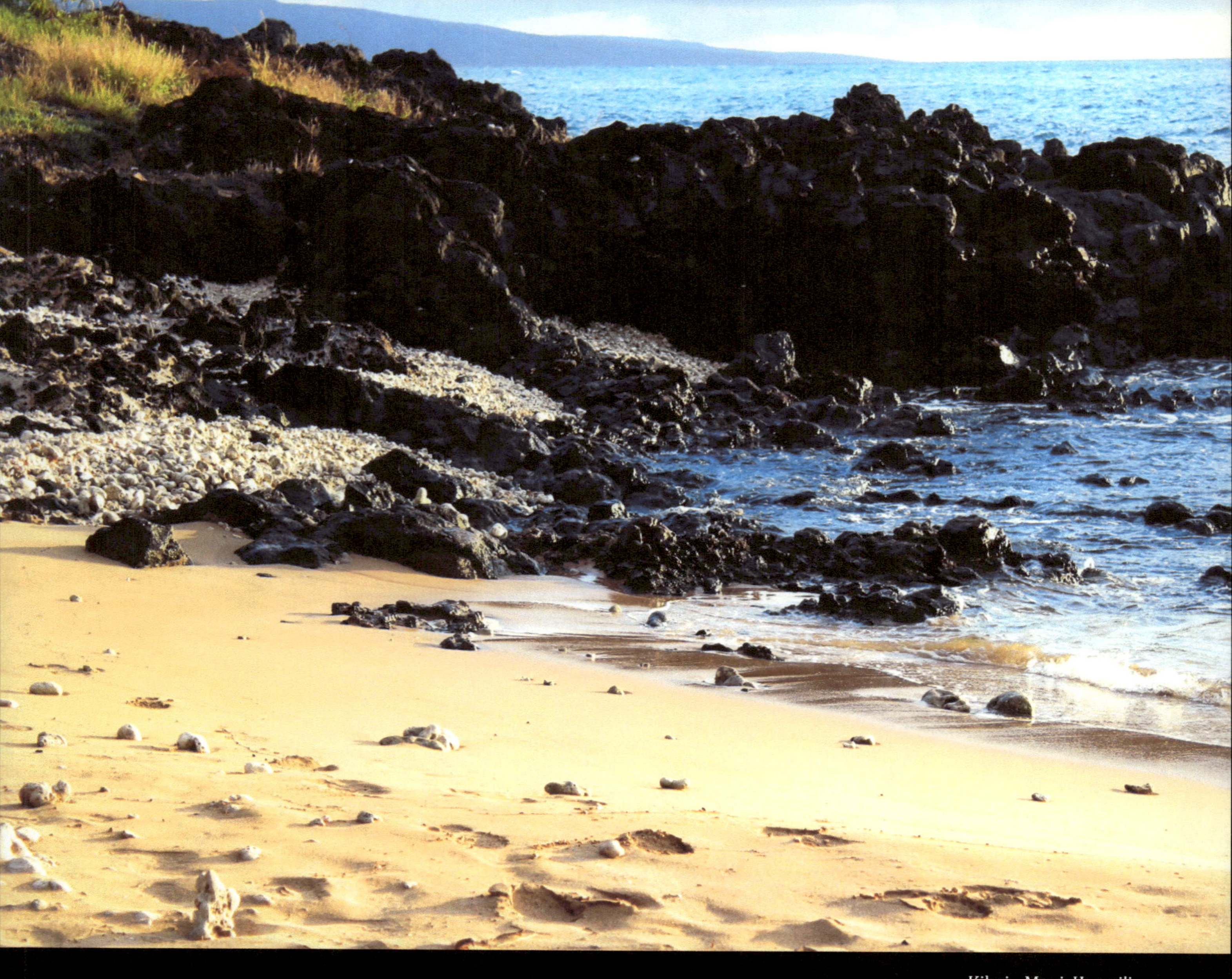

Kihei - Maui, Hawai'i

I Corinthians 13:1-3

Nothing is worth anything without love.

"I may speak with tongues of men and angels, but if I am without love, I have become like sounding brass or a clanging cymbal. And though I have the gift of prophecy, and understand all mysteries; know every hidden truth, and have all faith strong enough to move mountains - but have no love, then I am nothing. I may give away all I possess to feed the poor, or even give my body to be burned in sacrifice, but if I don't have love – then I have gained nothing."

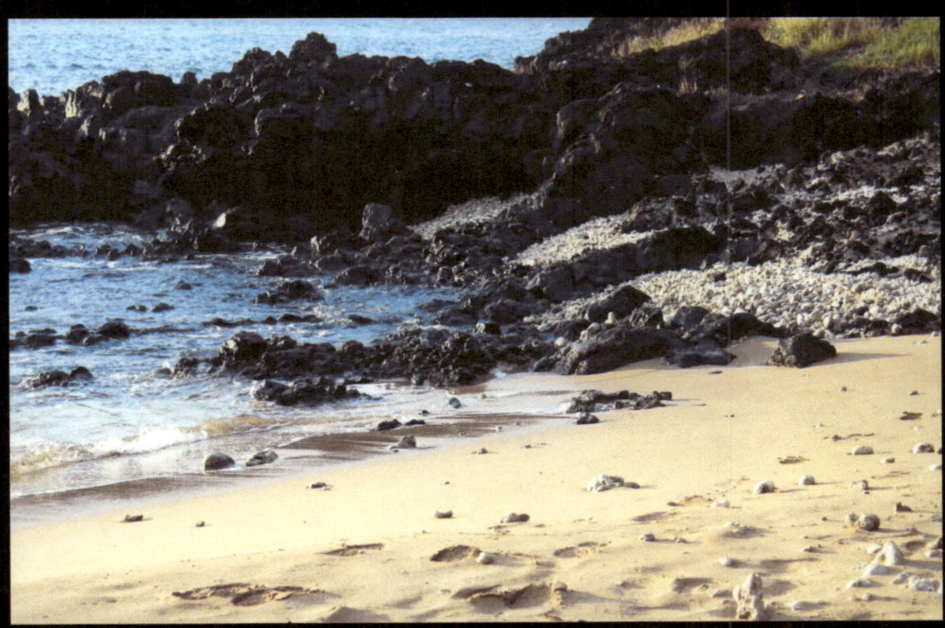

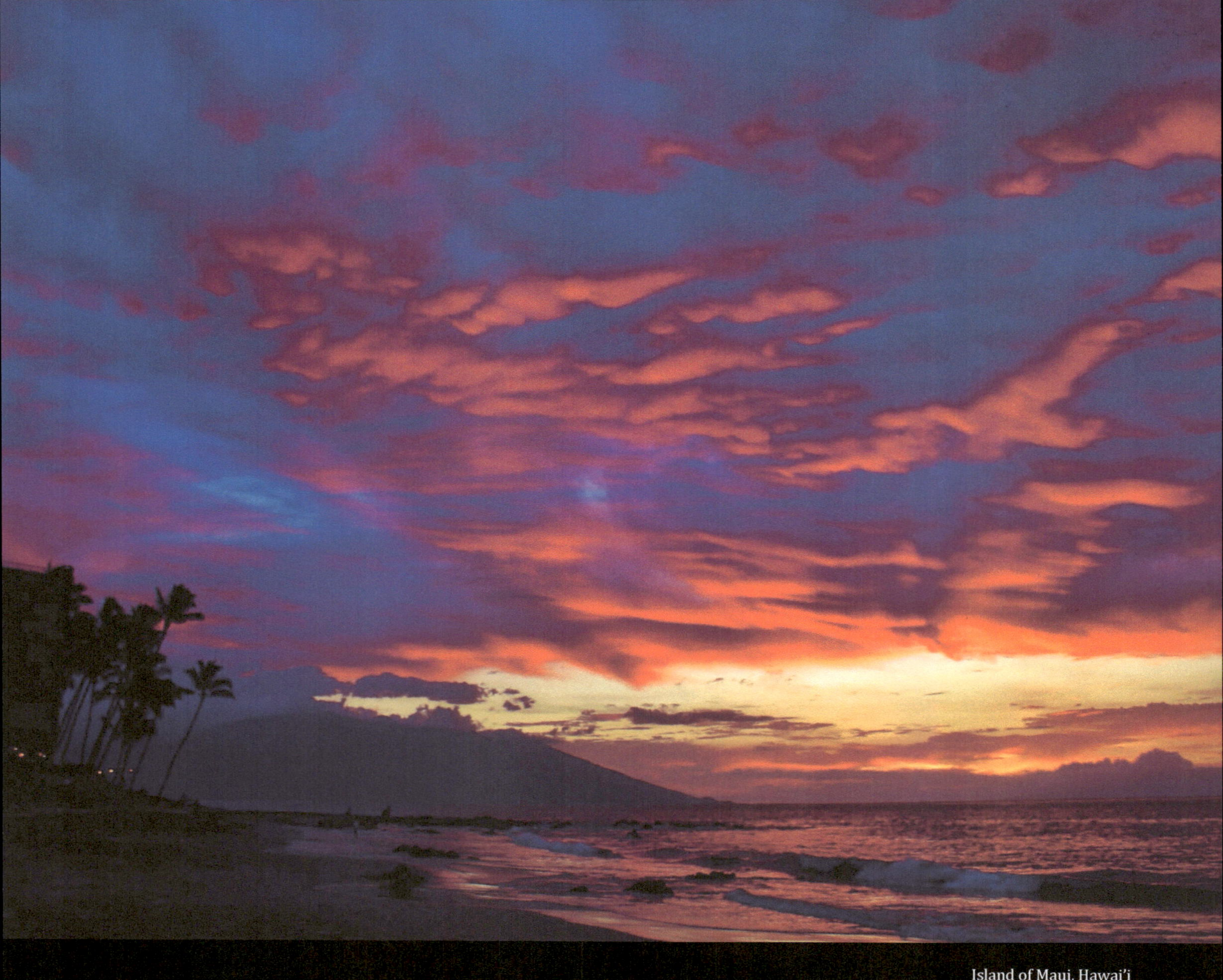

Island of Maui, Hawai'i

I Corinthians 13:4-13

Love is everything. Love never ends.

"Love suffers patiently and is kind. Love envies no one. Love is never boastful, nor conceited, nor rude. It is never selfish nor quick to take offense. Love keeps no score of wrongs. And it does not gloat over other men's sins, but delights in the truth. Love bears all things, believes all things, hopes all things, and endures all things. There is nothing love cannot face. There is no limit to its faith, its hope, and its endurance. Love never comes to an end, even when all testimonies stop, or all tongues cease to speak, or knowledge vanishes away. For we know only a part and can only foretell only a part, but when what is perfect has come, then all will be made clear. When I was a child, I spoke like a child, I had the understanding of a child, and thought like a child; but when I became a man, I put away childish things. Now we see through a dark glass, but then we shall see face to face. Now my knowledge is only partial; but then I shall know even as I am known. In a word, there are three things that last forever; faith, hope and love, but the greatest of them all is love."

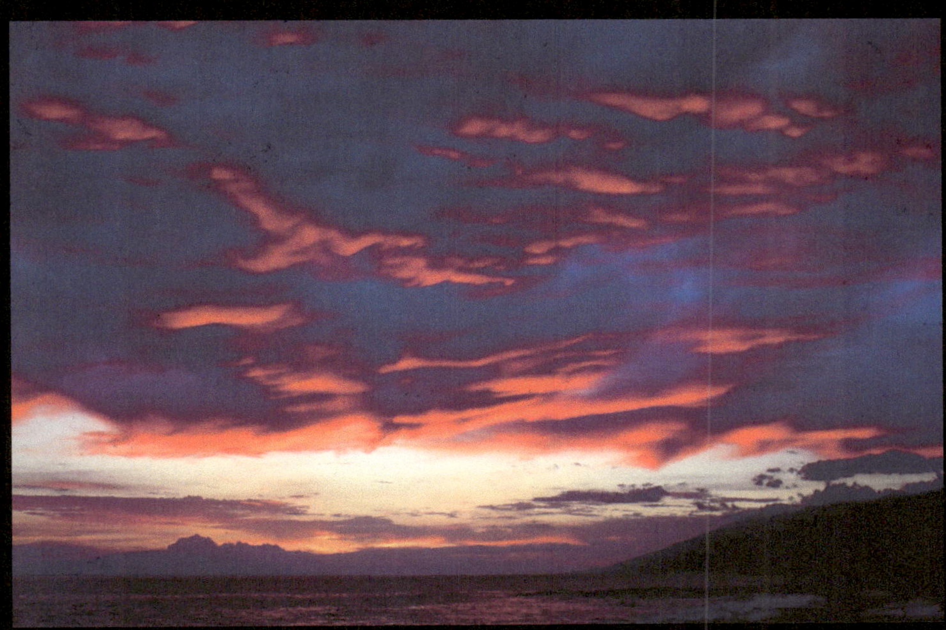

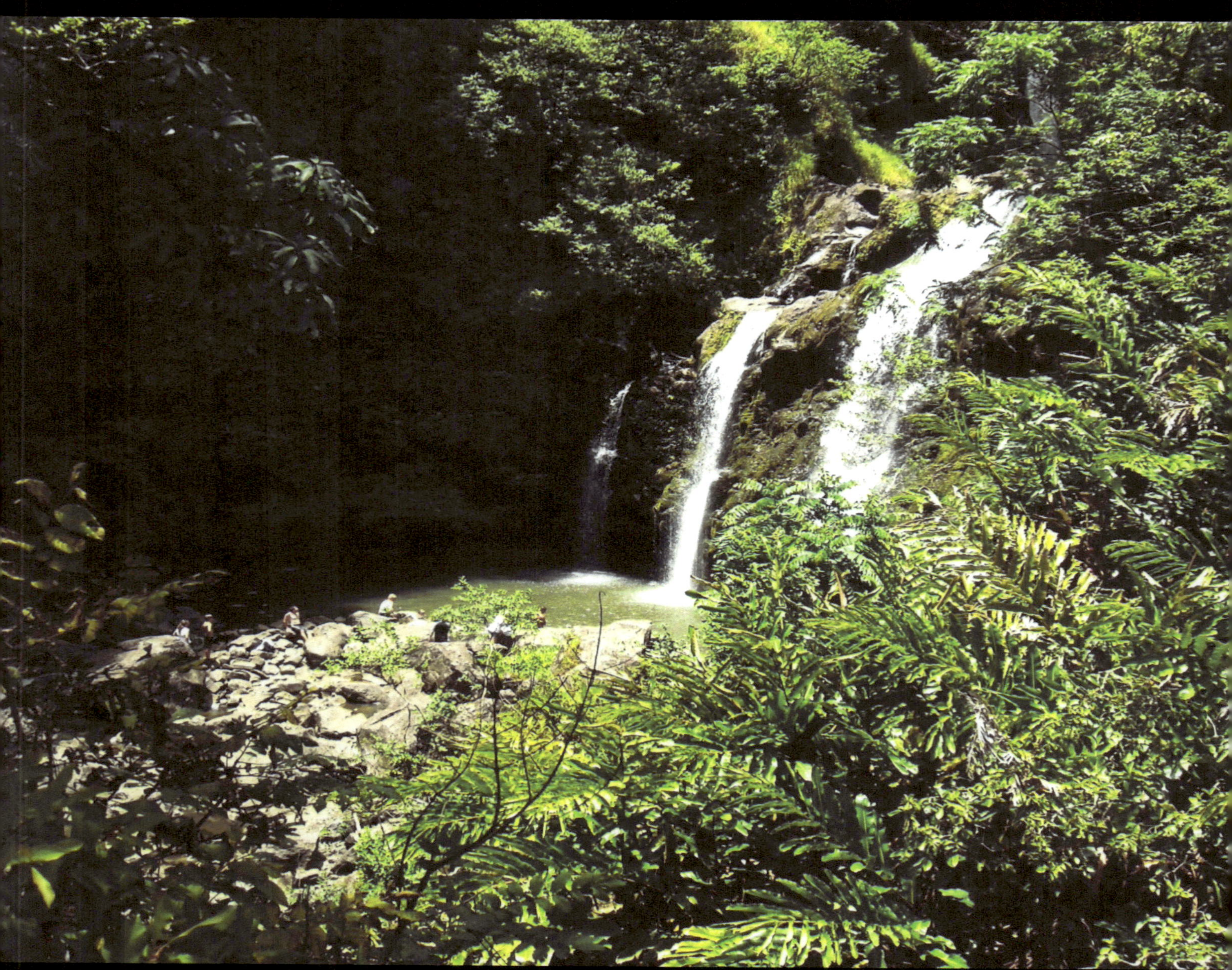

Road to Hana Waterfall- Maui, Hawai'i

Mark 5:36

Believe and don't be afraid…

There is nothing GOD cannot do.

"When Jesus heard the words that were said, He turned to the leader of the synagogue and said, ' Do not be afraid; believe."

(Jesus Christ)

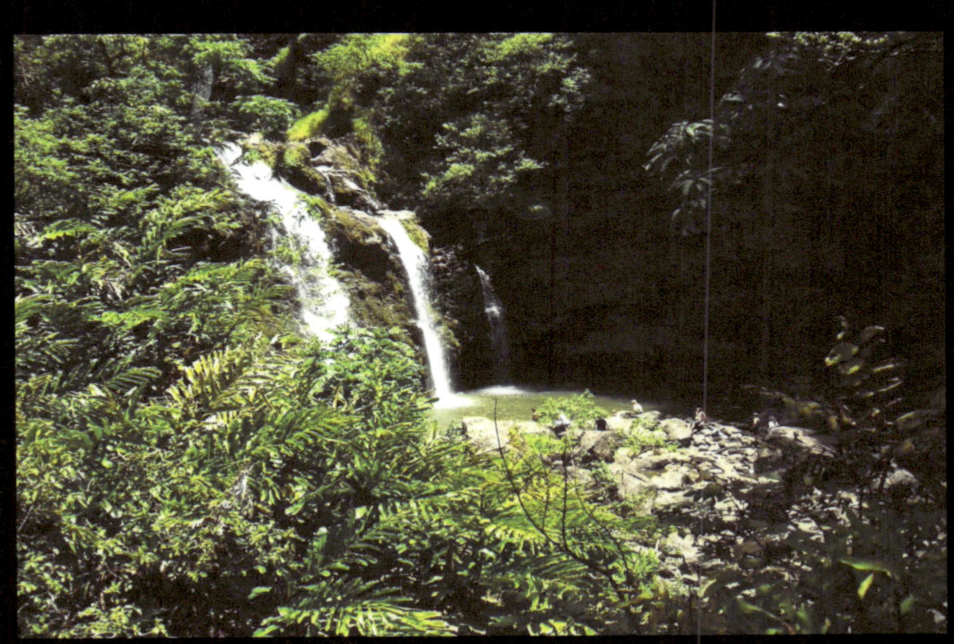

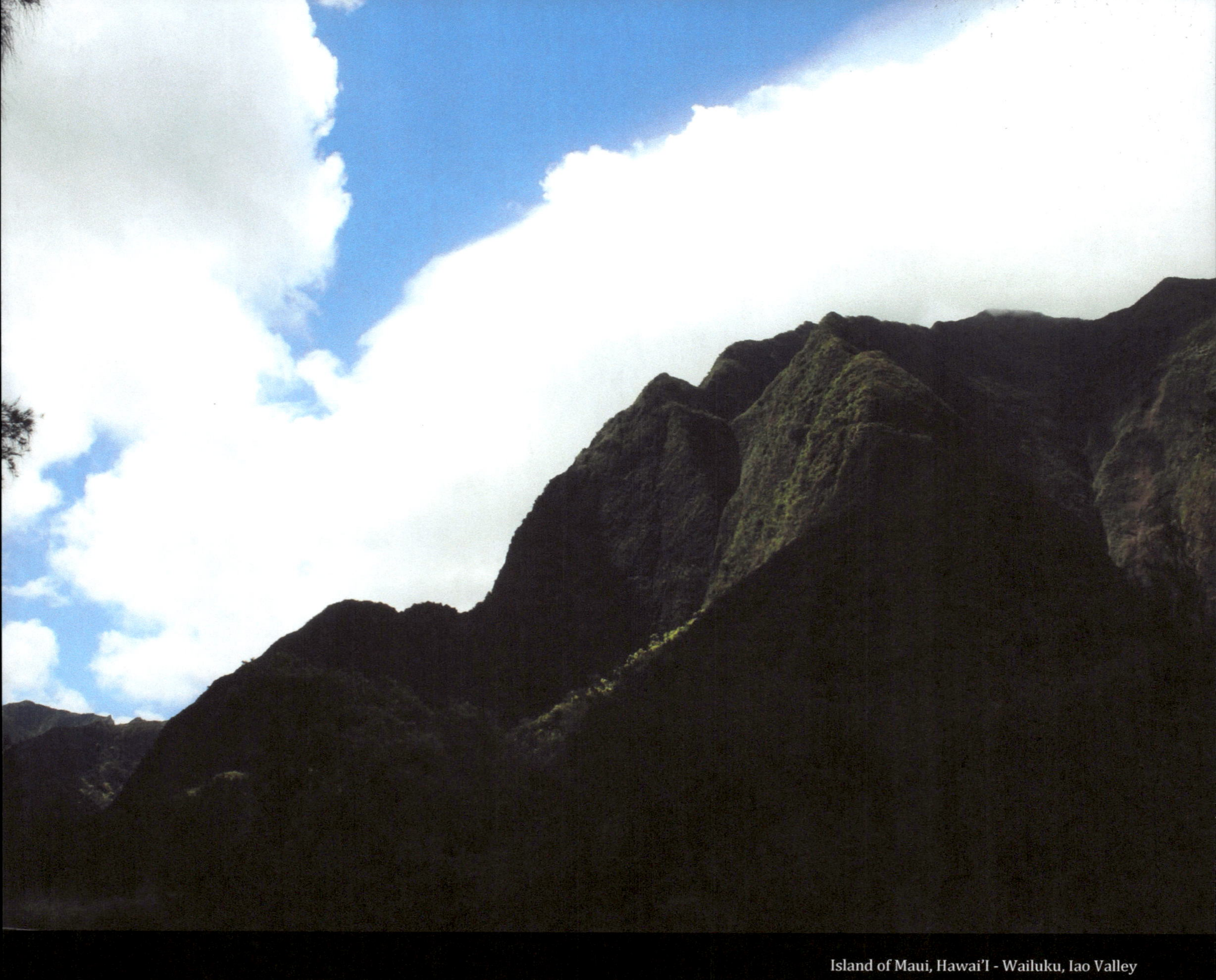

Island of Maui, Hawai'I - Wailuku, Iao Valley

John 14:27

The Divine gives you peace in your heart and mind.

"Peace I leave with you. My peace I give to you, such as the world cannot give. Don't let your heart be troubled, nor let it be afraid."

(Jesus Christ)

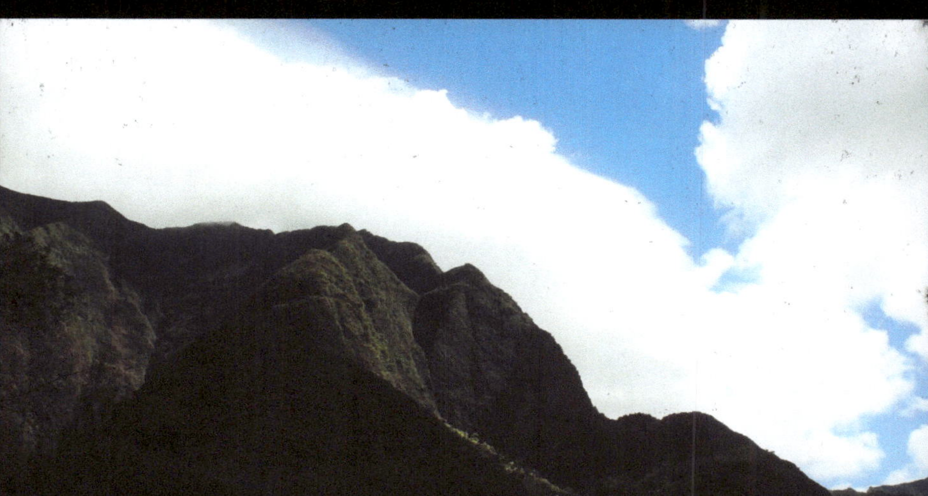

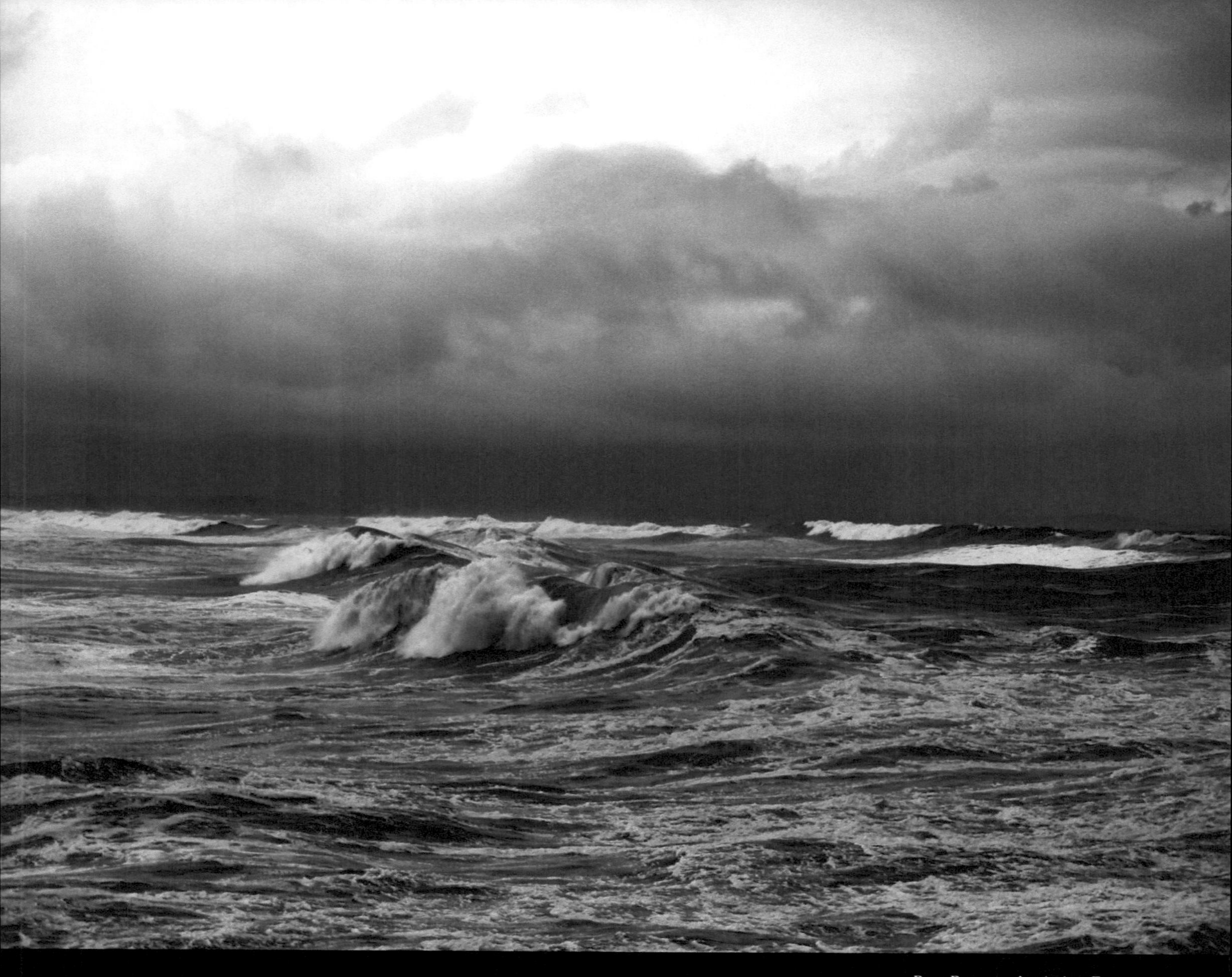

Pays Basque - Aquitaine, France

Isaiah 43:2

Through fire, the rain, and the stormy seas,

GOD will see you through.

"When you travel through the seas, I will be with you. And when you pass through the floods, they will not overtake you. And when you walk through the very fire, you shall not be burned, neither will the flames set you on fire."

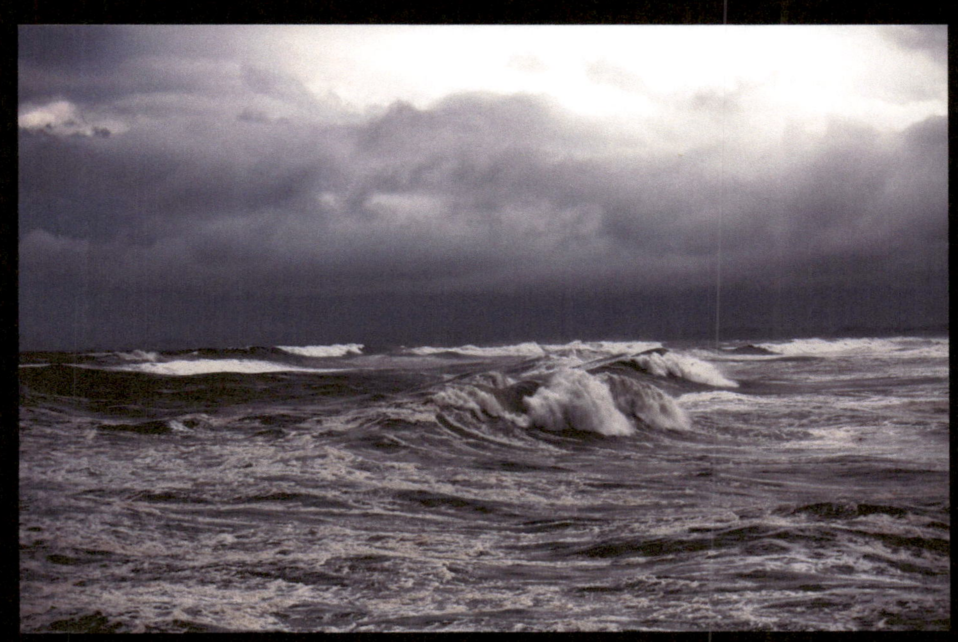

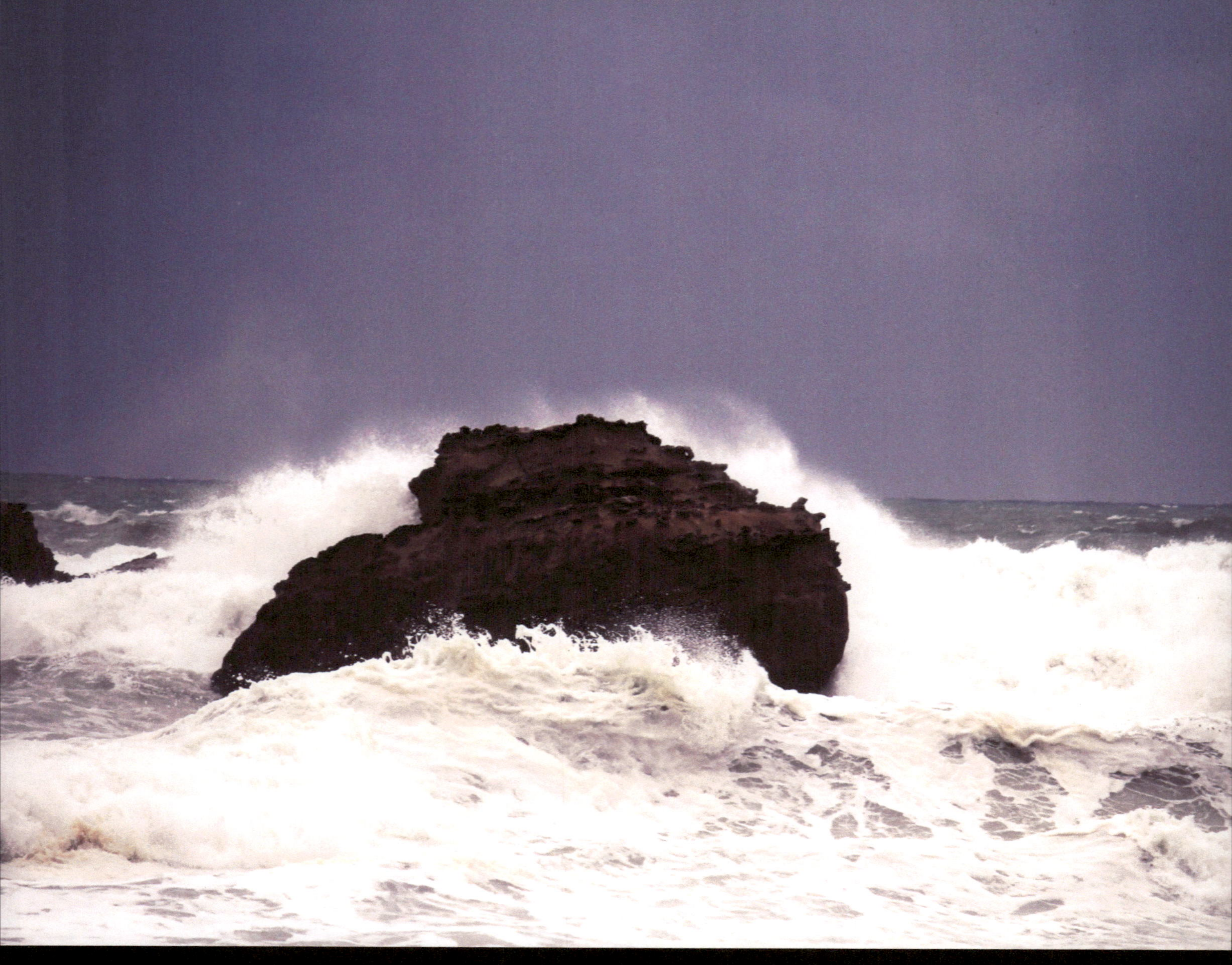

Pays Basque -Biarritz, France

Deuteronomy 31:6, 8

Be strong and courageous for GOD is with you.

"Be of a positive spirit and be strong. Do not worry or be afraid of any person, because GOD Himself goes with you, and He will not fail you, nor abandon you. The Divine personally walks in front of you. He is by your side. Never be afraid or discouraged."

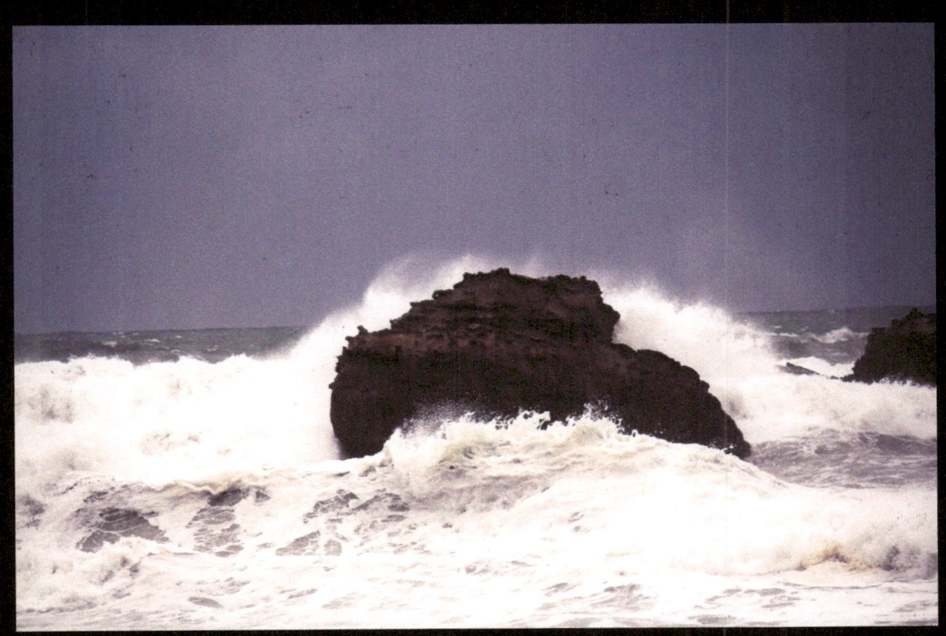

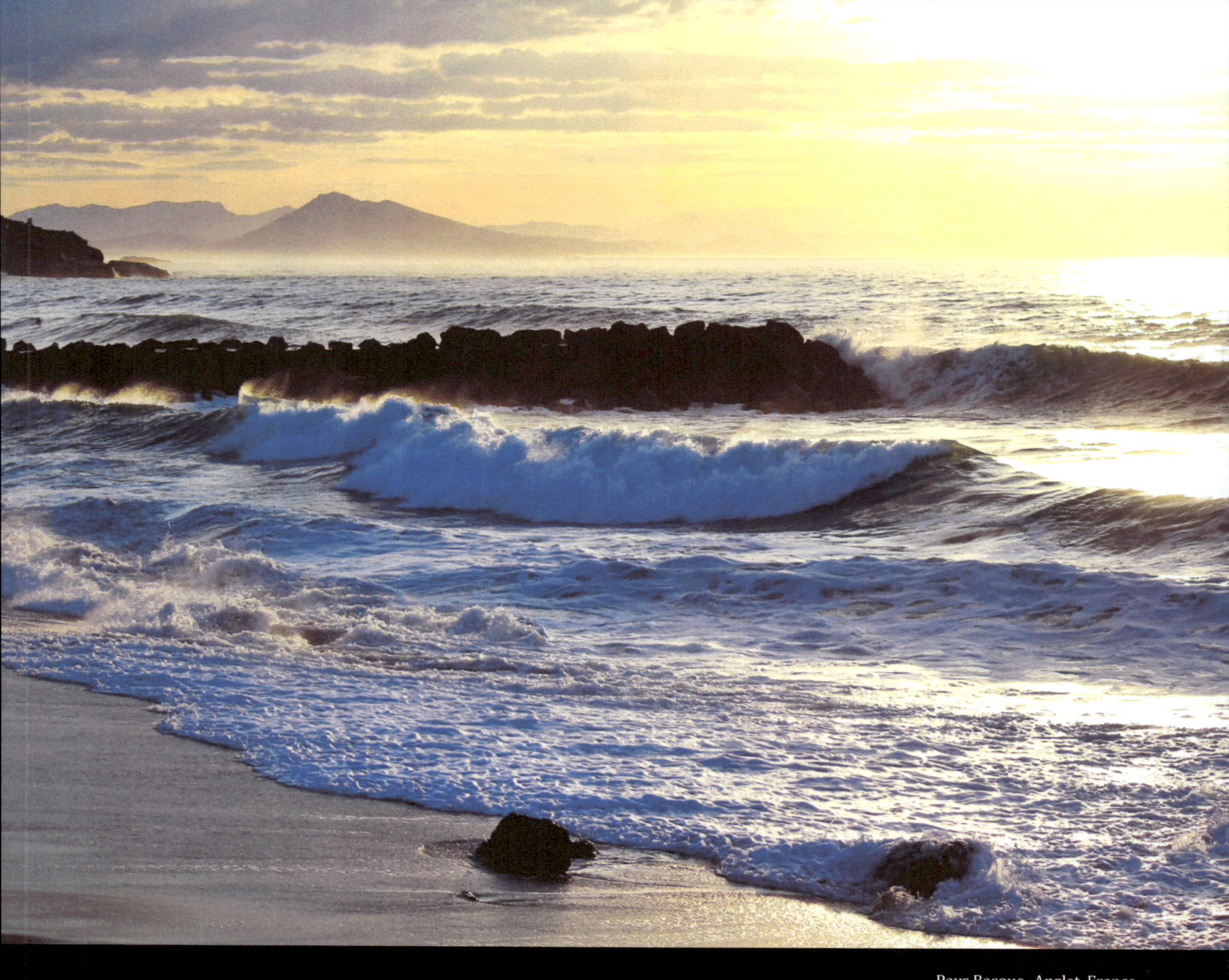

Pays Basque -Anglet, France

"I will deliver you... And you shall not be given into the hands of those who made you afraid. For I will surely deliver you, and you shall not fall victim to the sword; but your life will be a gift to you, because you trusted in Me."

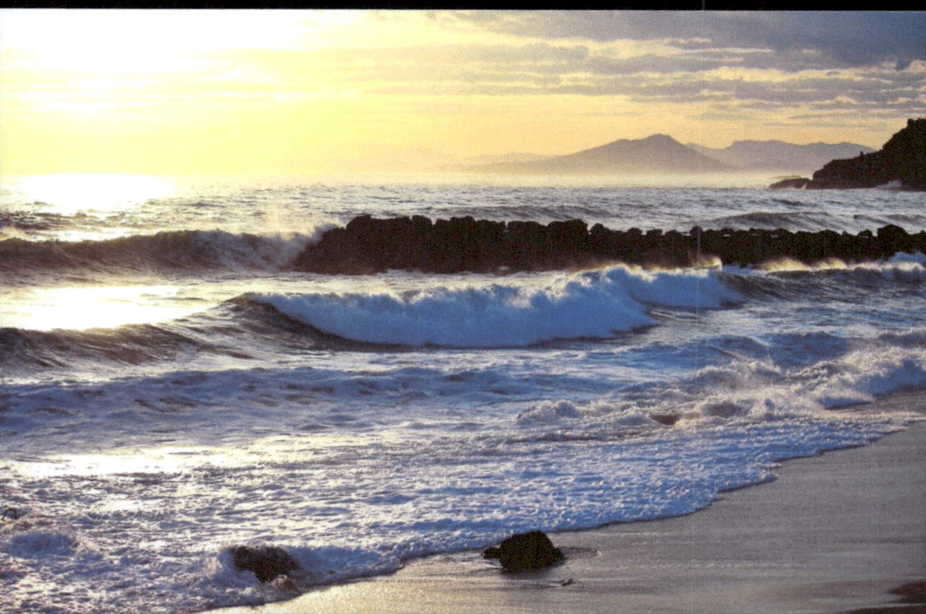

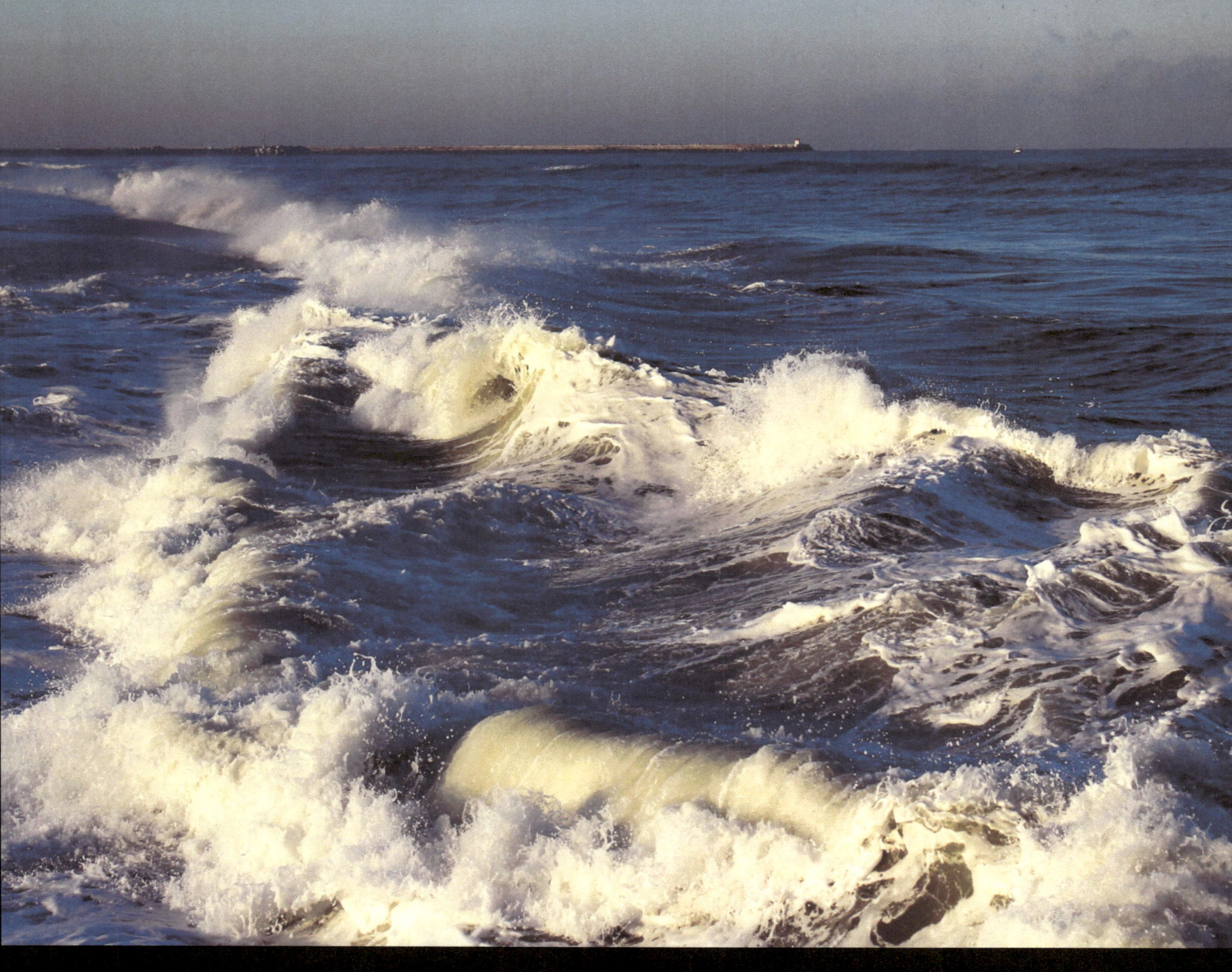

Pays Basque -Anglet, France

Philippians 4:13

There is nothing you can't do.

You stand on the power of GOD.

"I can do ALL things with the help of Christ, who strengthens me."

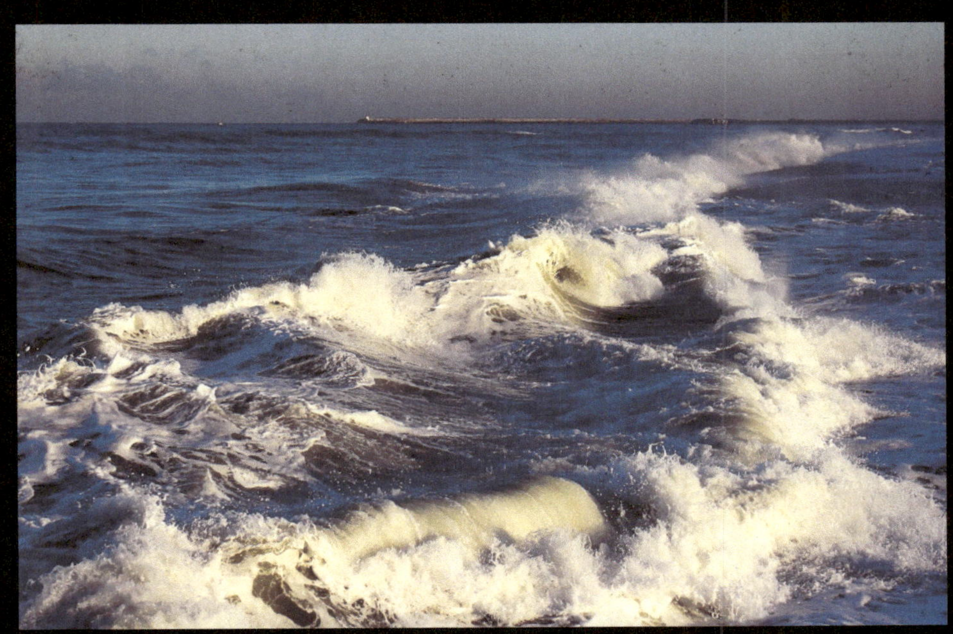

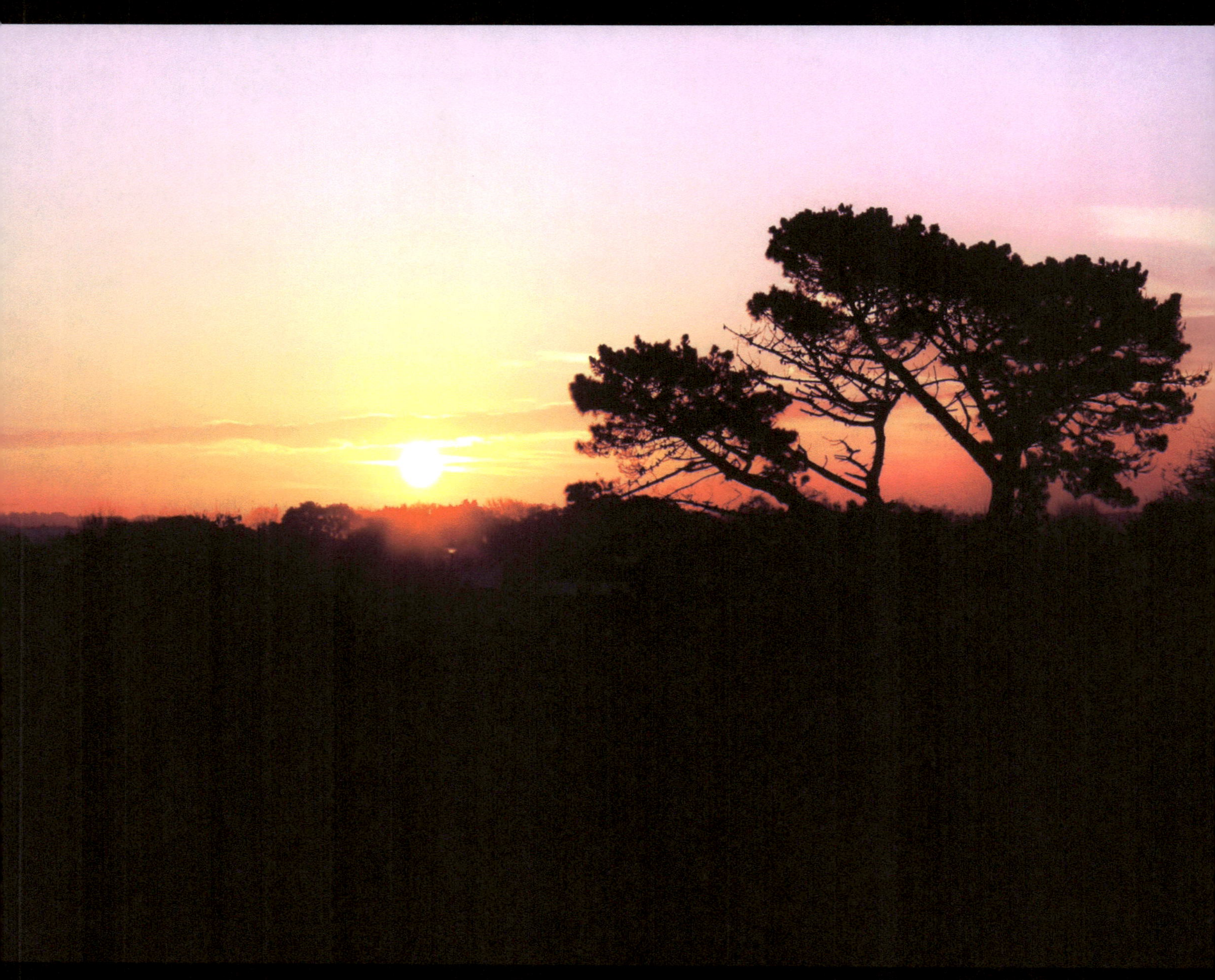

Sunrise in Anglet, France

1 John 4:7-8

Never be afraid to love and never be ashamed that you loved, for true love comes from GOD. Love is Divine.

"My Beloved, let us love one another, for love comes from GOD. And everyone that loves is born of GOD and knows GOD. But a person who doesn't love, does not know GOD; for GOD is LOVE."

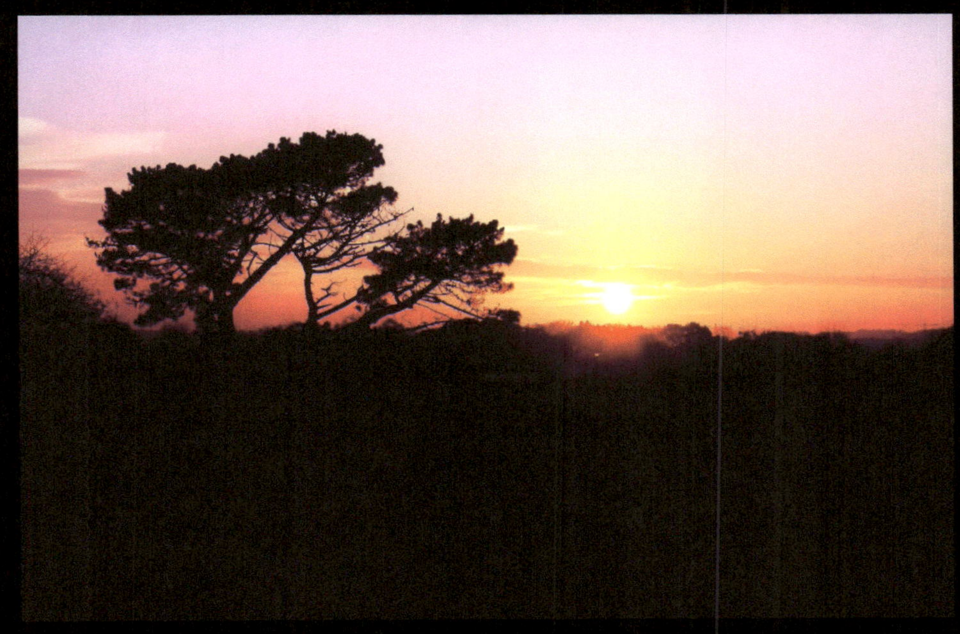

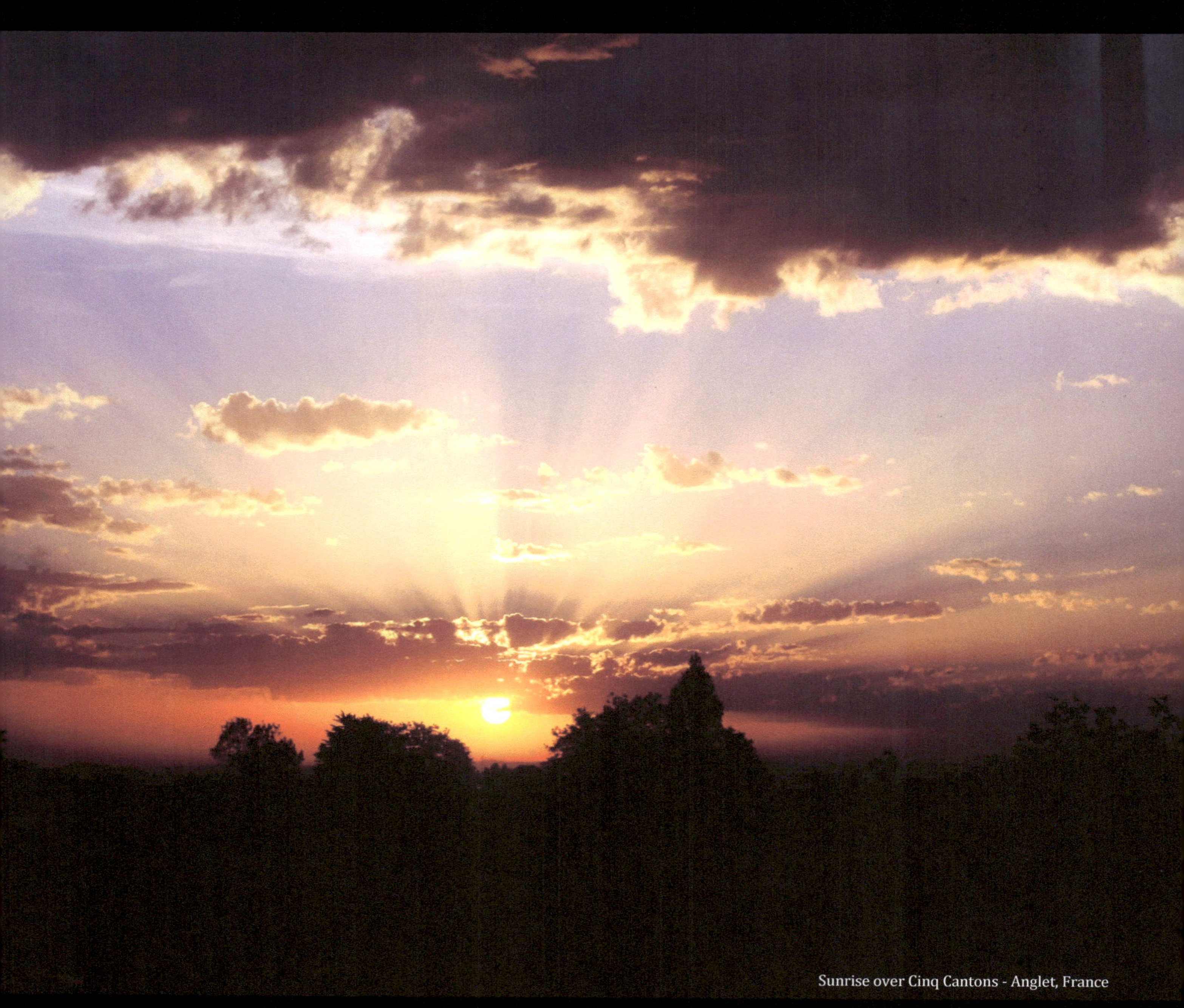

Sunrise over Cinq Cantons - Anglet, France

Micah 7:8

You shall overcome; even the darkness.

"Do not think that you can gloat over me, my enemies; even though I have fallen, I will rise! And if ever I sit in a place of darkness, The LORD shall be my light."

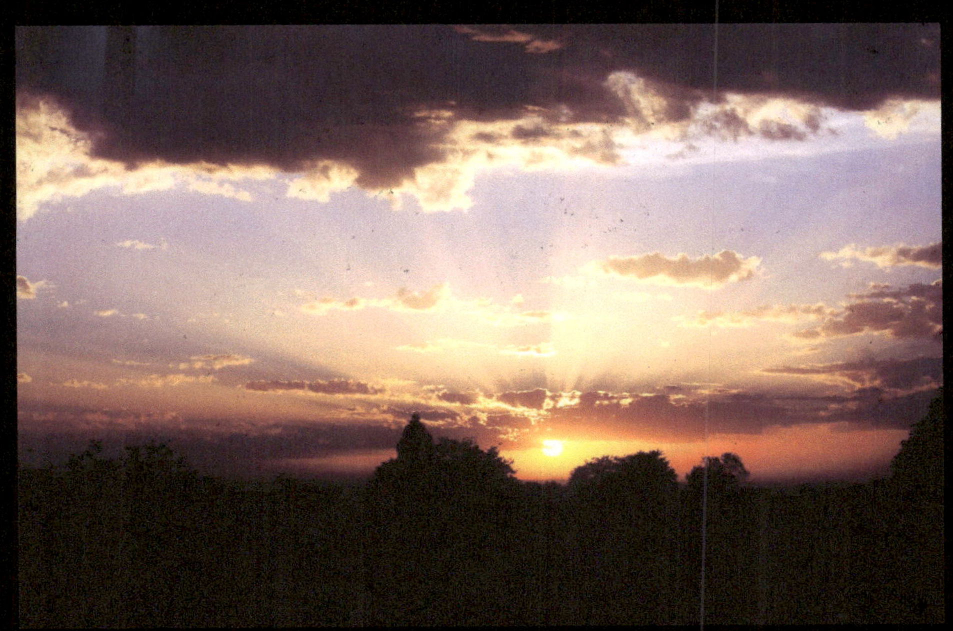

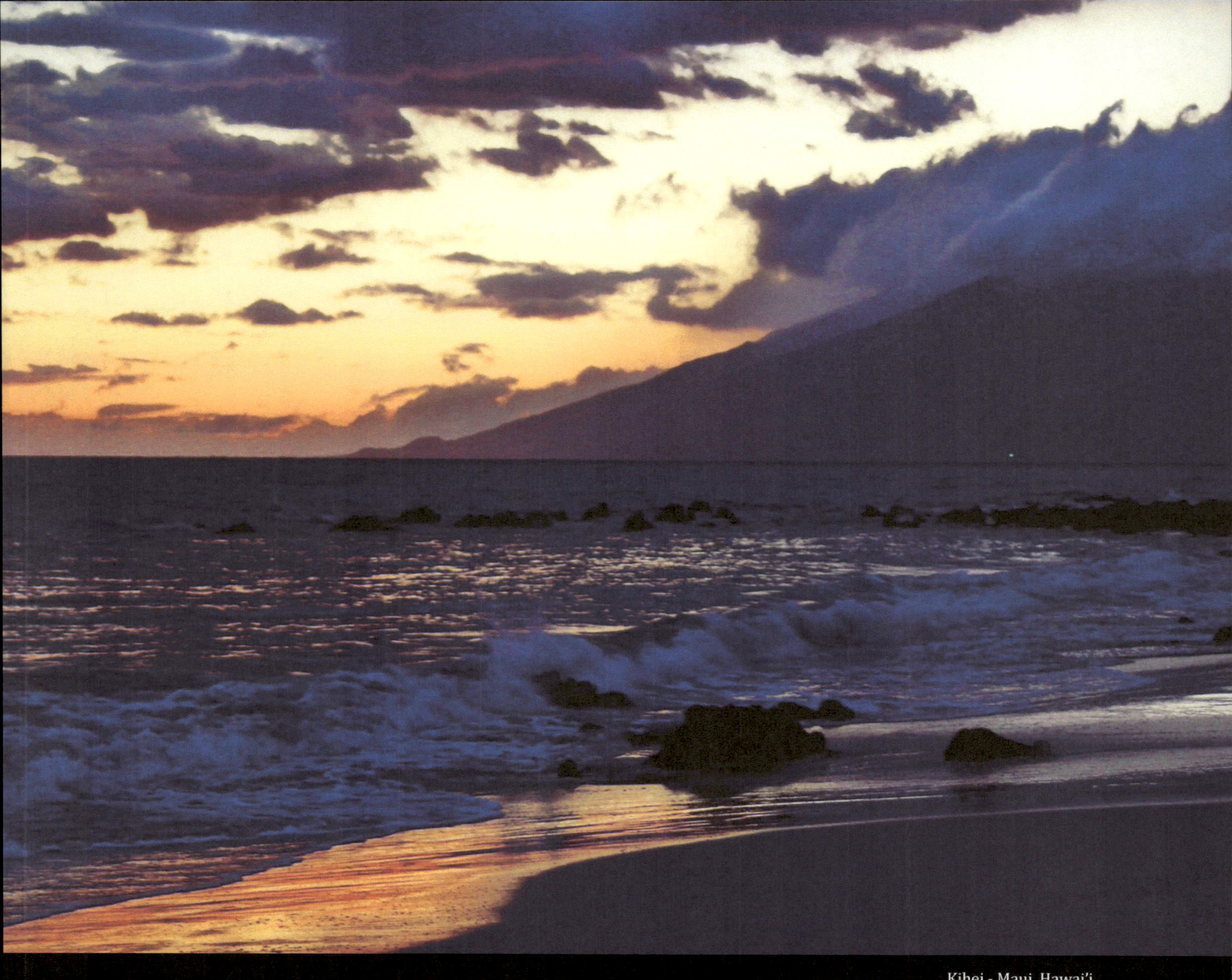

Kihei - Maui, Hawai'i

Mathew 9:28-29

The Divine will give you what you believe.

"'...Do you believe that I have the power to do what you want?" "Yes, sir," they said. Then he touched their eyes and said, "As you have believed, so let it be," and their sight was restored."

(Jesus Christ)

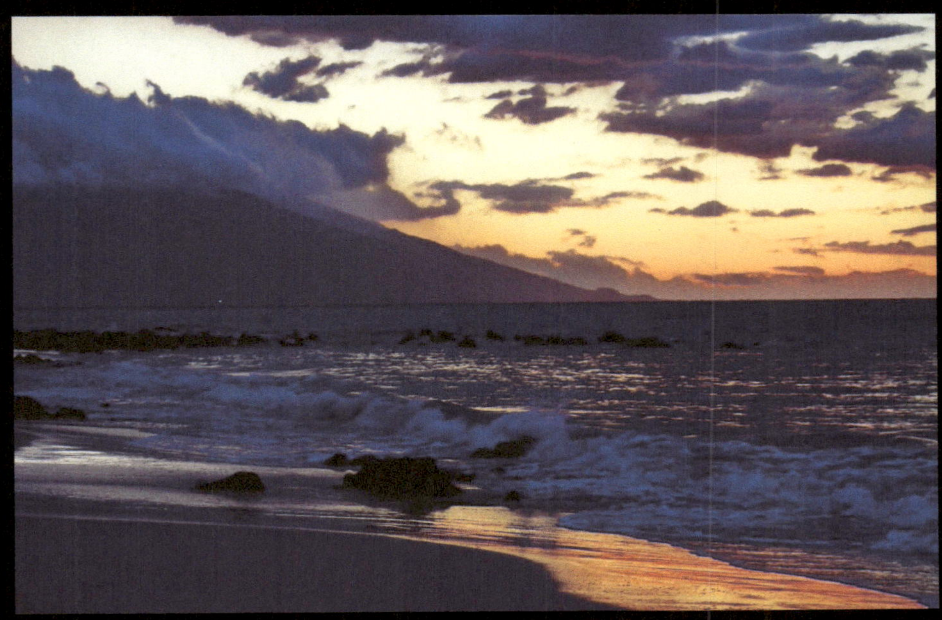

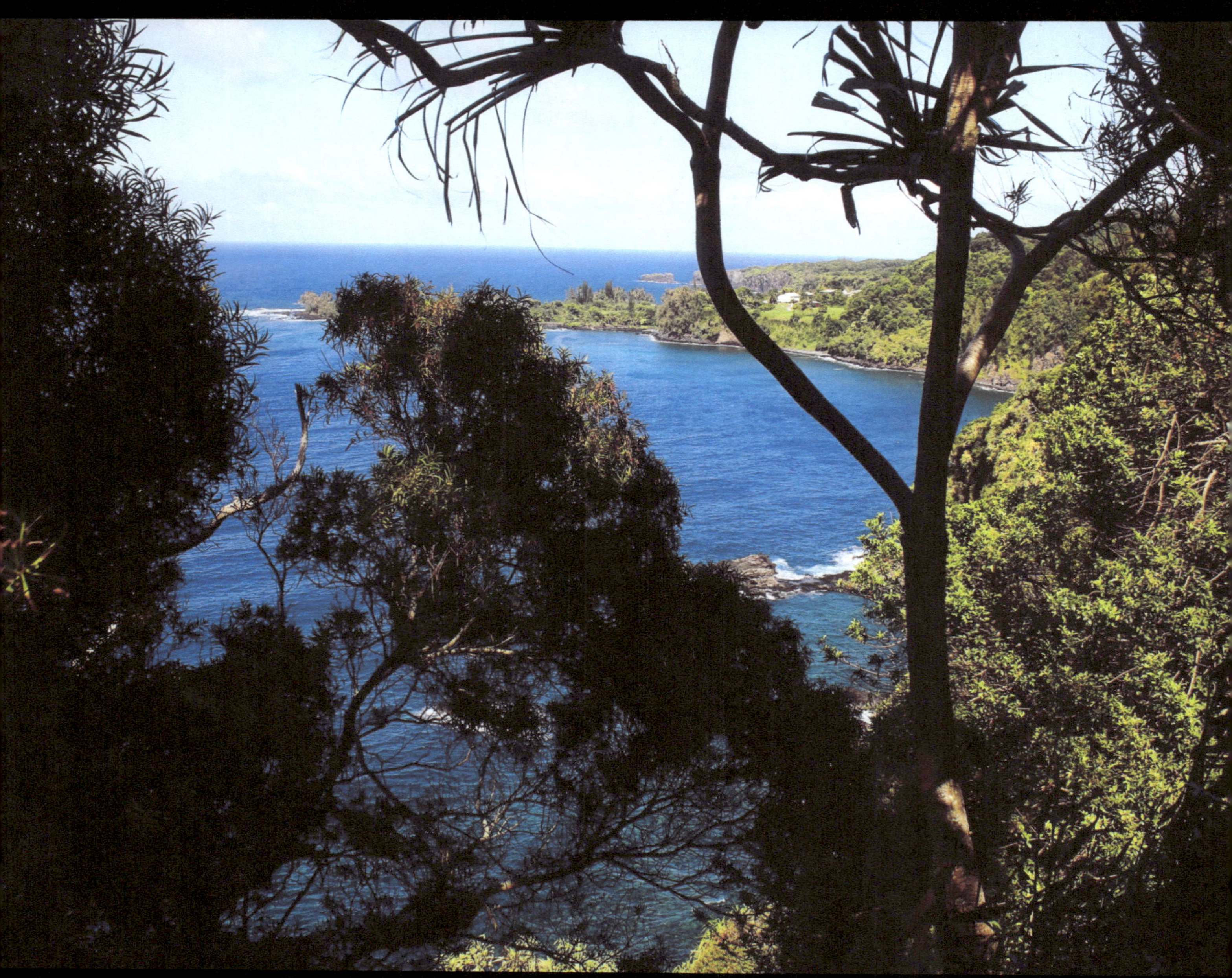

Hana - Maui, Hawai'i

Revelation 21 :3-4

Wipe away your tears, for The LORD your GOD is with you and will make everything brand new.

" I heard a voice from heaven shouting that the House of GOD was in the midst of men and that He was living with them. And they shall be His people and GOD himself shall be with them. GOD shall wipe away all the tears from their eyes, and there shall be no more dying, nor sadness, nor weeping, and no more pain, because all these things will have passed away. Behold, for I will make ALL things new."

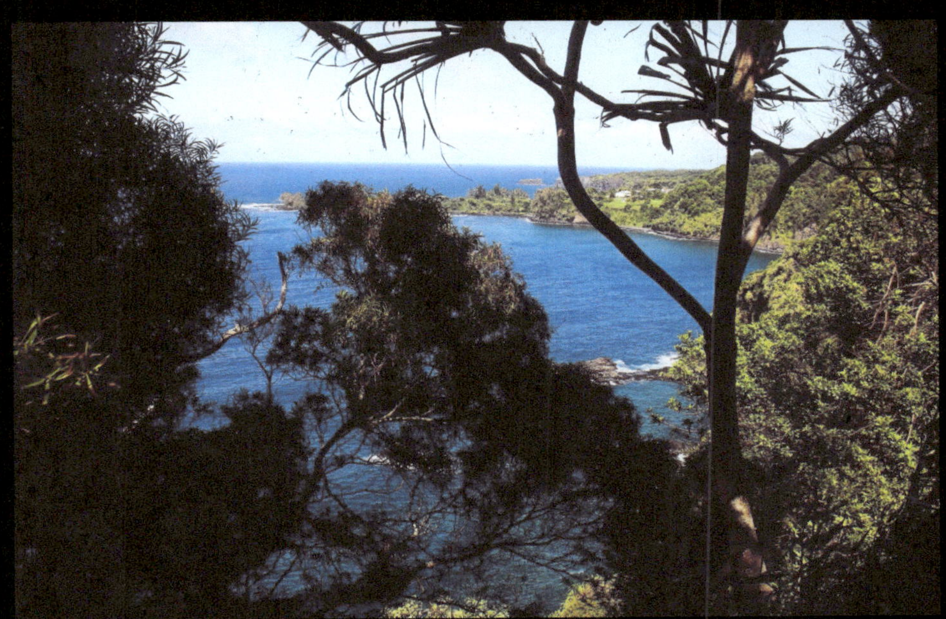

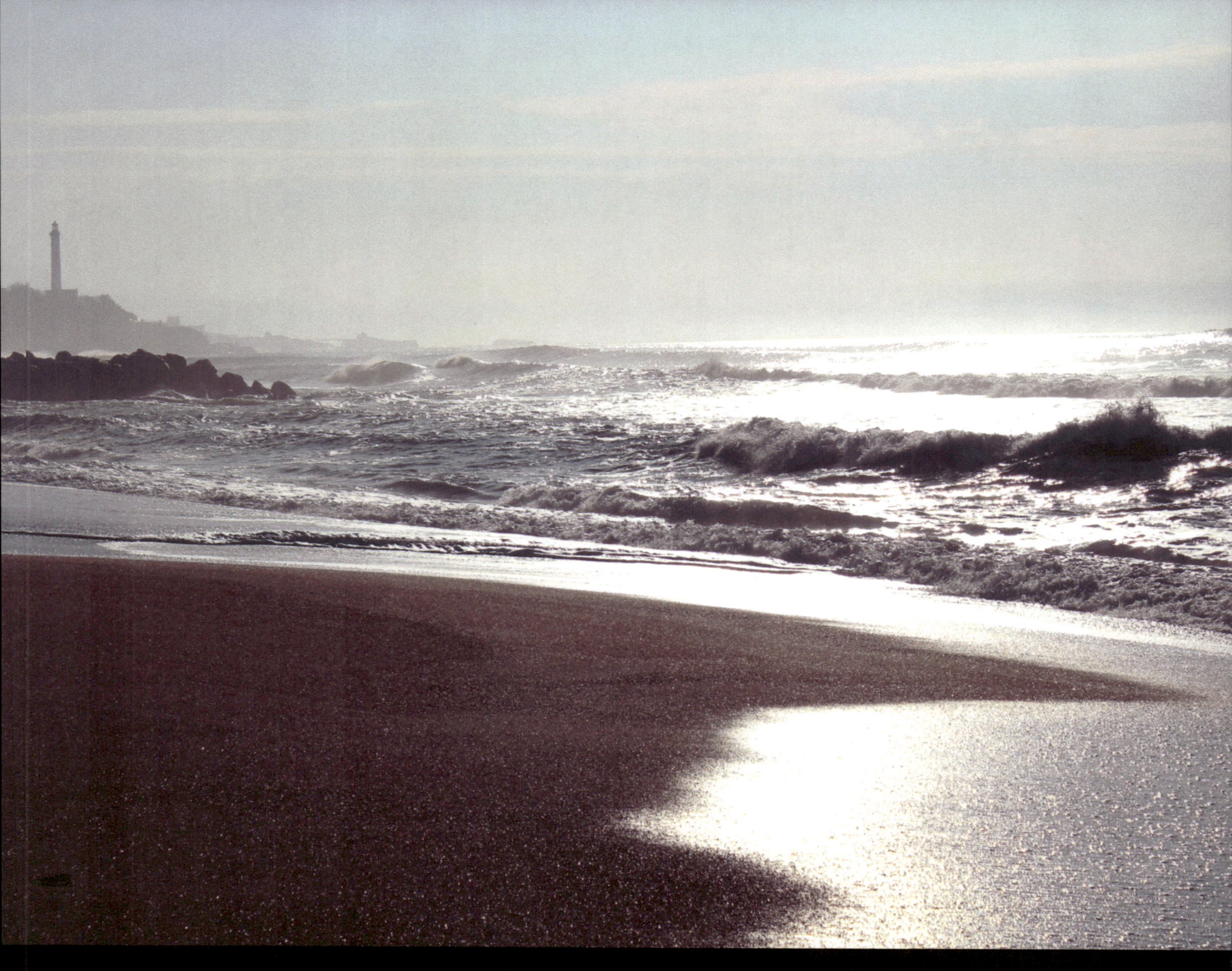

Chambre d'Amour - Anglet, France

Joshua 1:9

You never go through any trial alone.

The Divine is forever with you.

"Have I not commanded you, telling you to be strong and positive, to be courageous, not disheartened and not afraid? For I the LORD your GOD will be with you wherever you go."

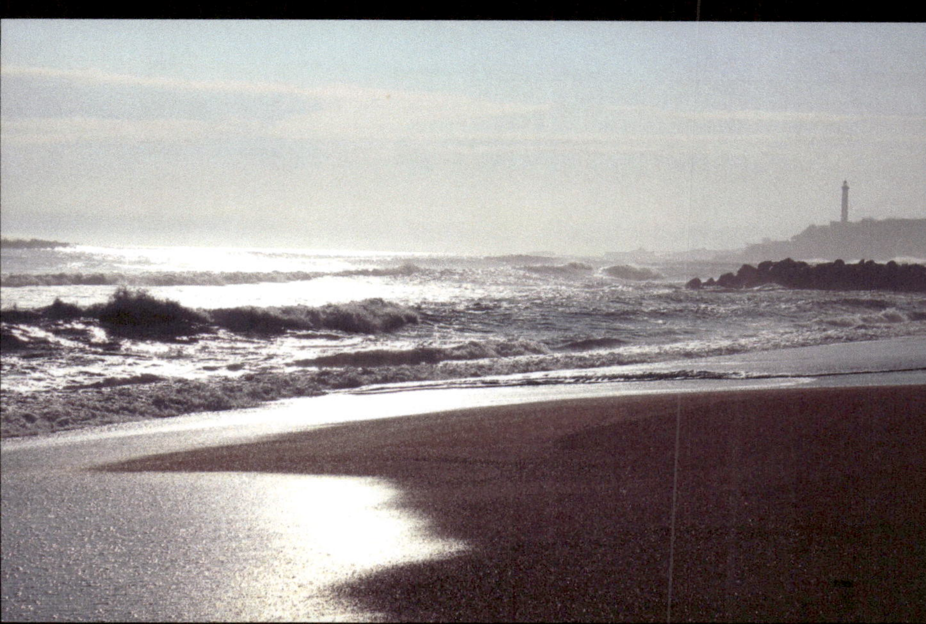

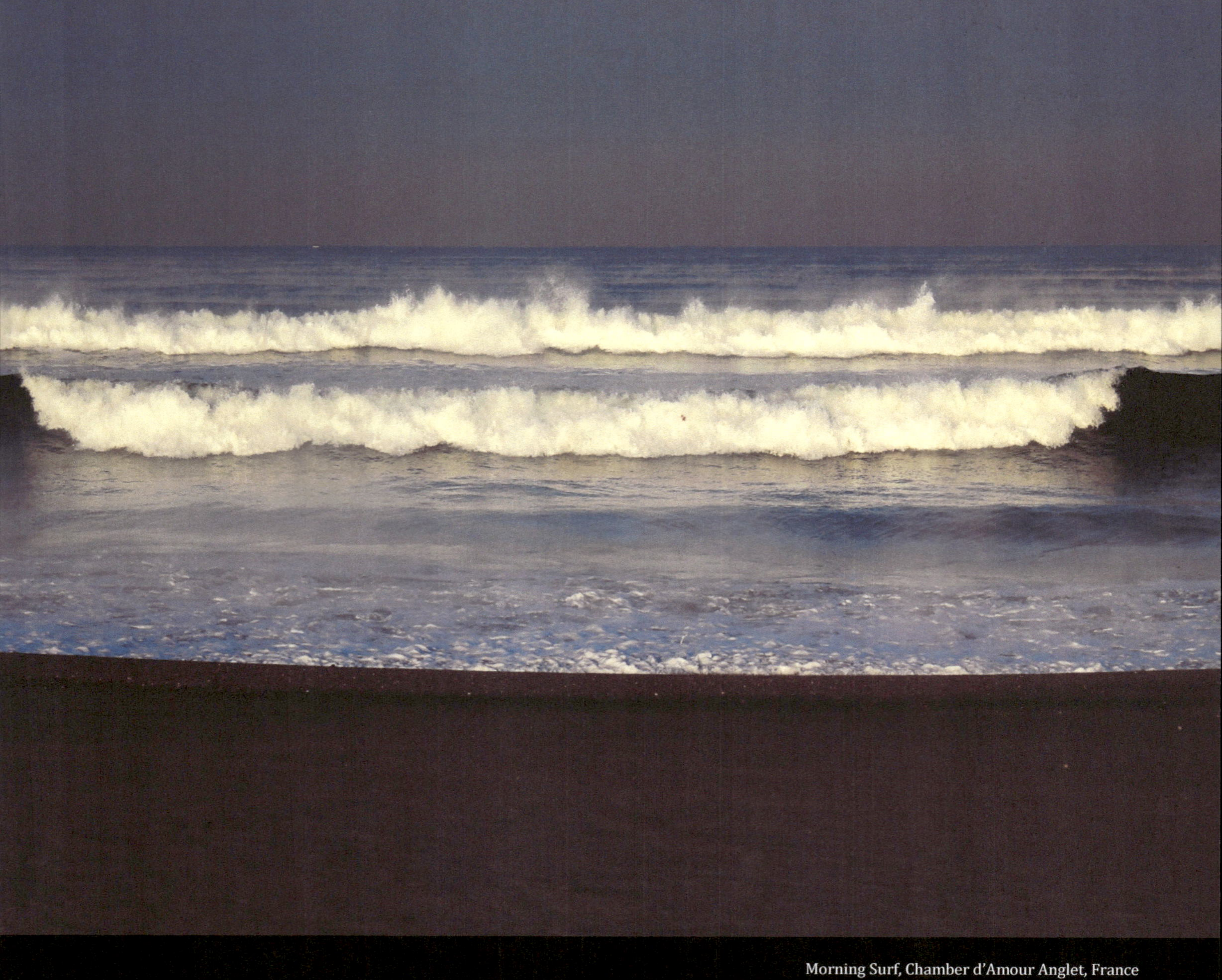

Morning Surf, Chamber d'Amour Anglet, France

"No one will be able to stand against you, through all the days of you life, for I will be with you as I was with Moses. I will not leave you, nor ever fail you."

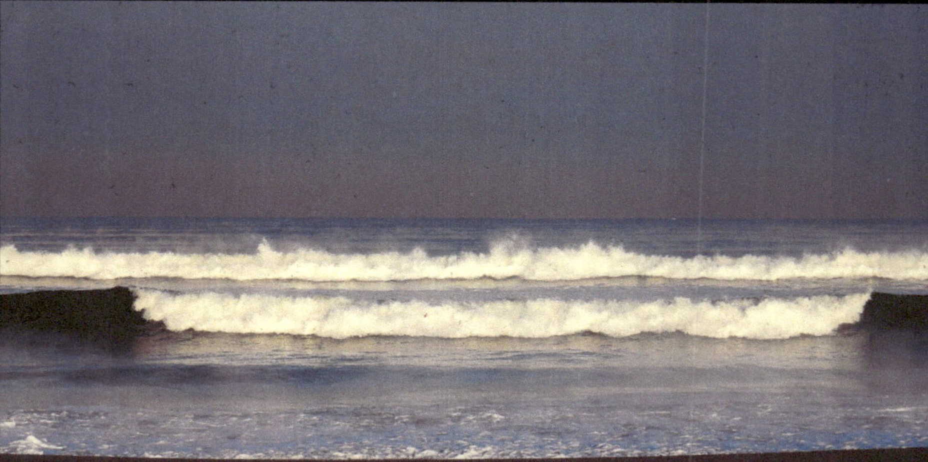

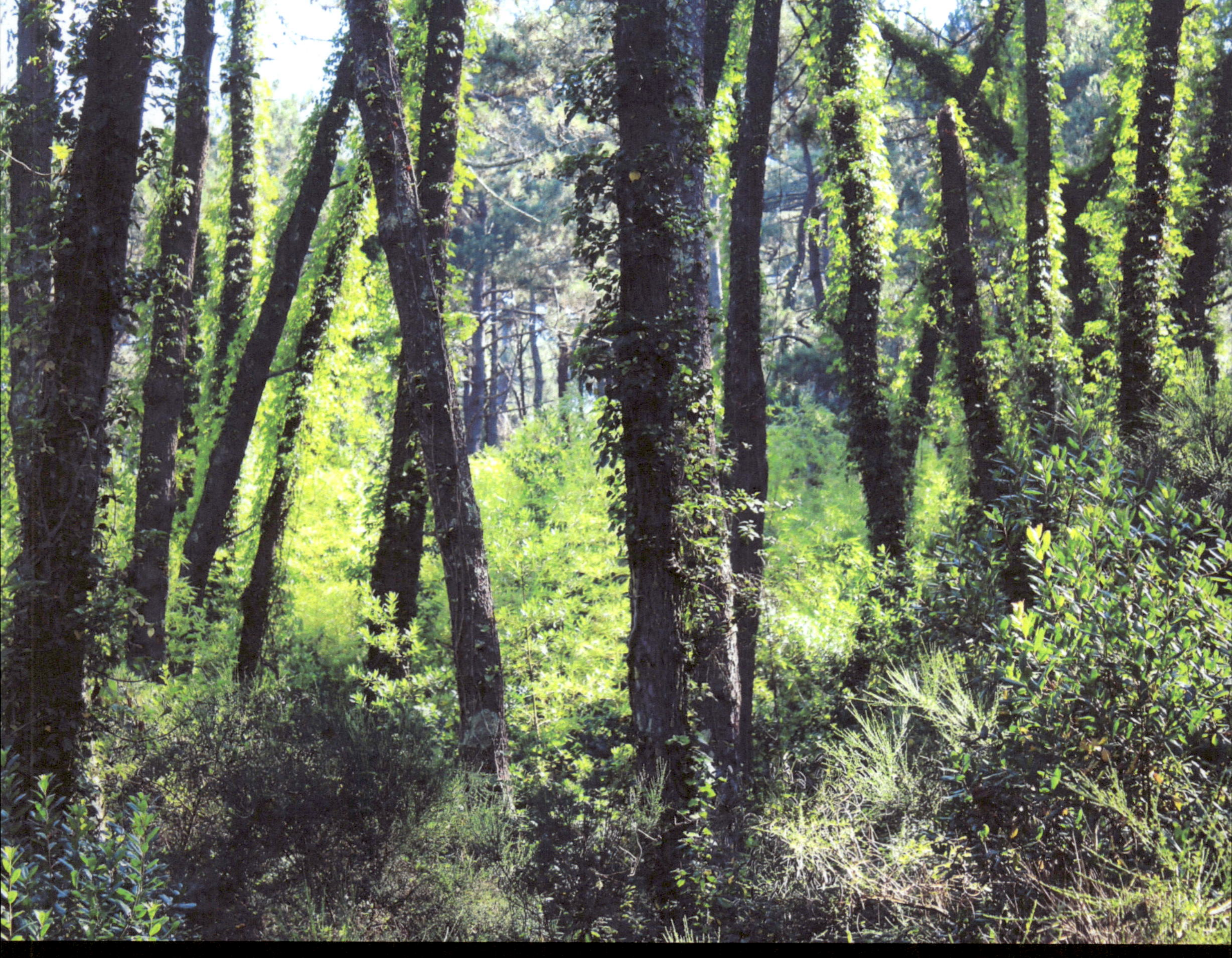

Forêt de Chiberta - Anglet, France

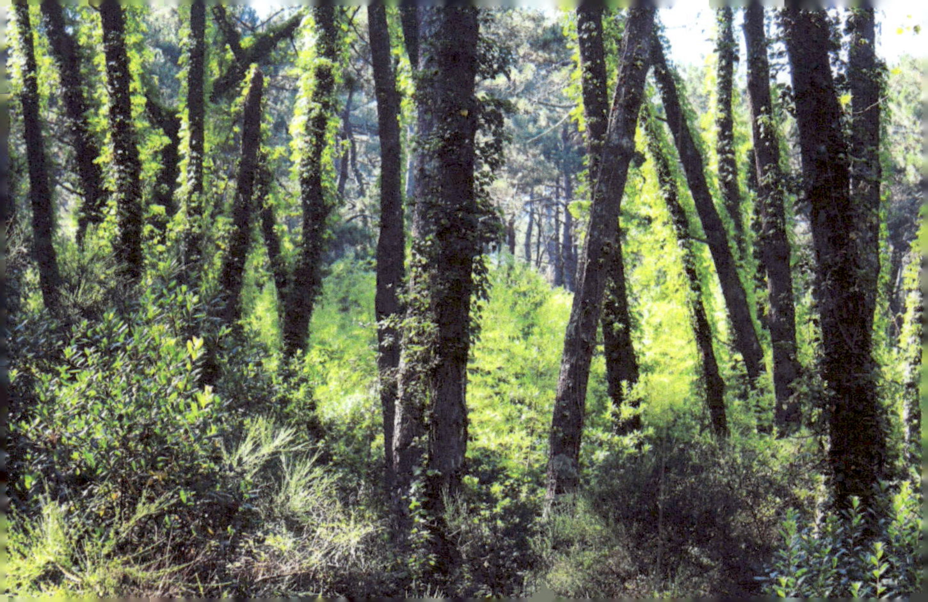

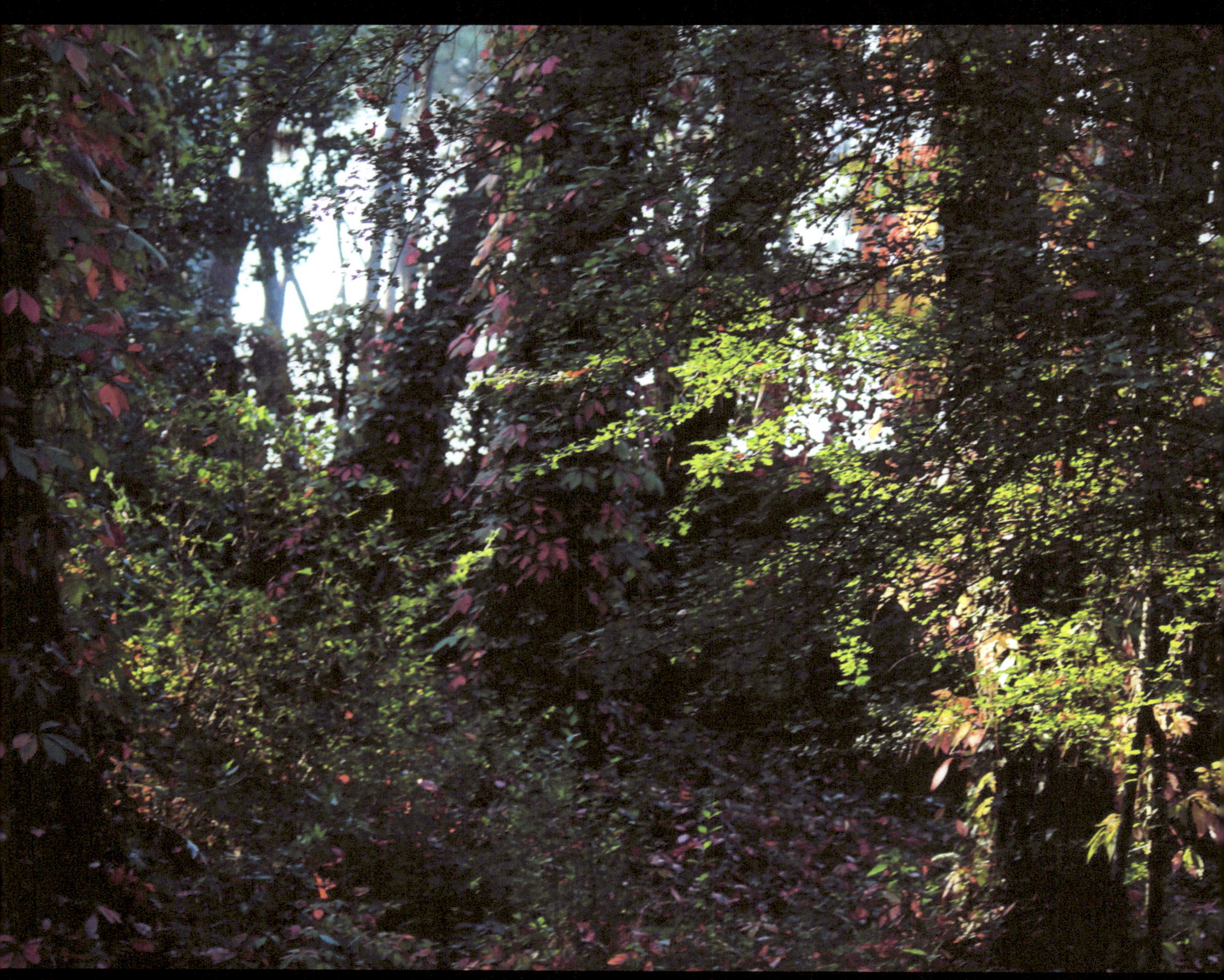

Forêt de Chiberta - Anglet, France

Psalms 49:5 & Psalms 62:7

Fear no man… Trust in GOD.

"Why should I be afraid in the evil days when cruelty and hate surrounds me and is nipping at my heels? GOD is my salvation and my glory. He is my rock, and my strength. I trust in GOD."

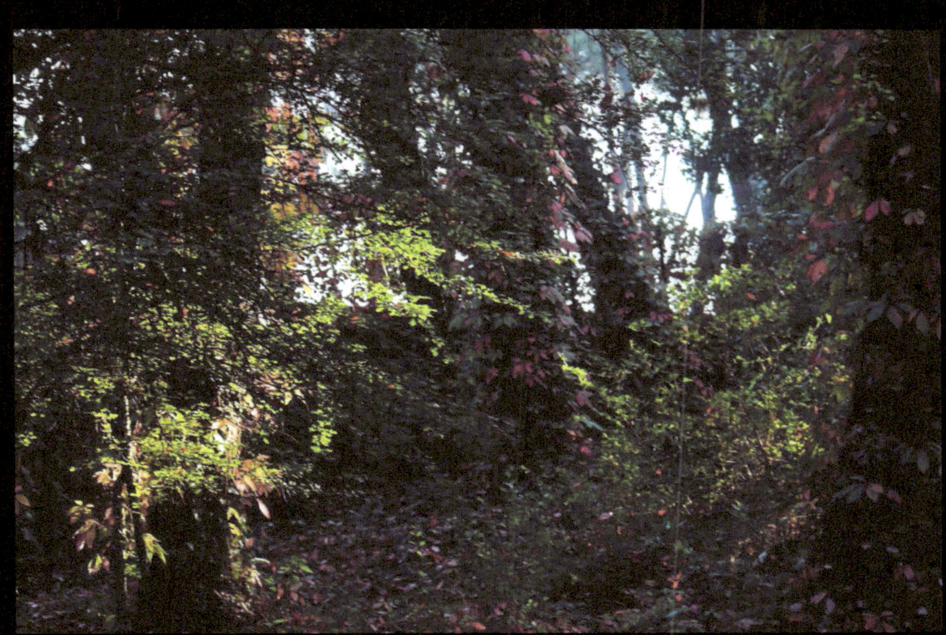

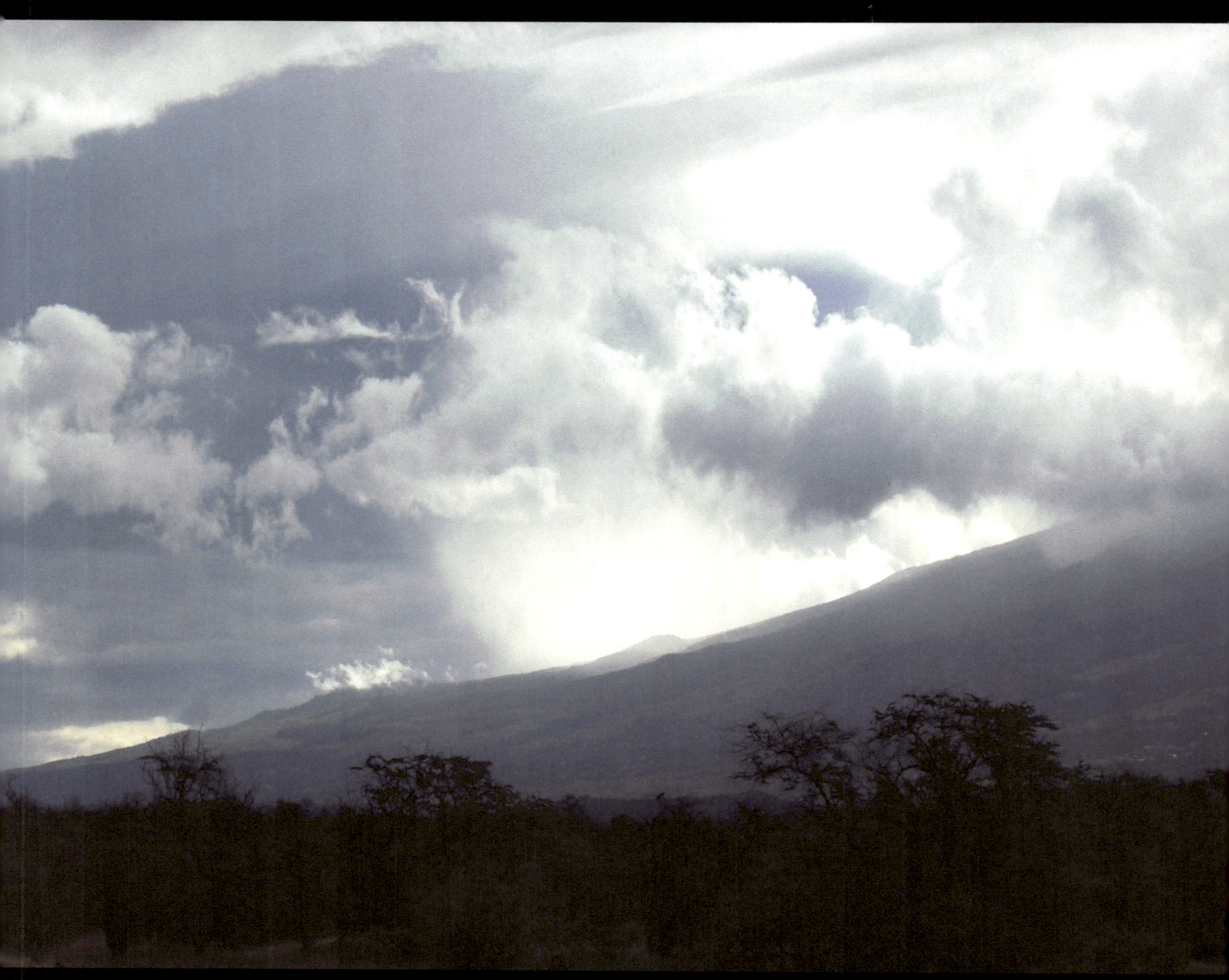

Island of Maui, Hawai'i

Mark 11:22-24

Have faith in the Divine and believe you have the power to manifest.

"Have faith in GOD. For as sure as I say to you, whoever tells this mountain, 'Move and fall into the sea' and do not doubt in their heart, but believes that what he says will happen, he will manifest whatever he says. Therefore I tell you, whatever you ask for when you pray, believe that you receive it."

(Jesus Christ)

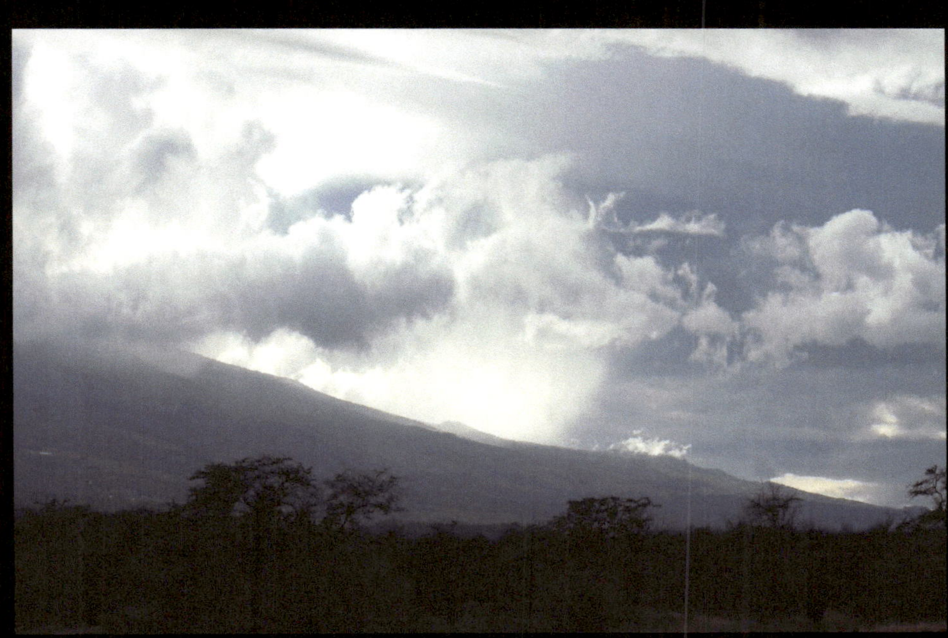

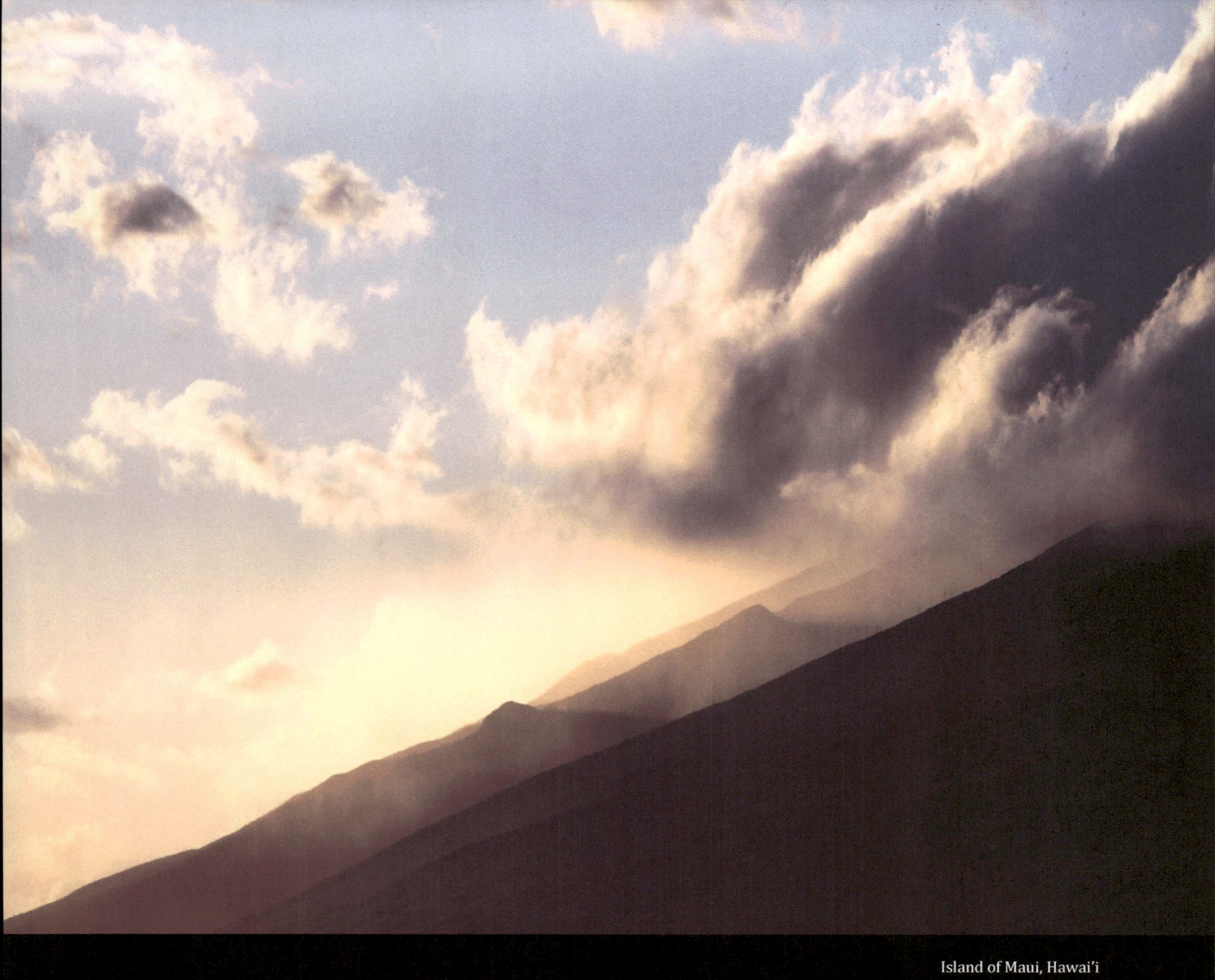

Island of Maui, Hawai'i

Hebrews 10:32-36, 39

Have confidence even when you've suffered loss.

"...You met the challenge of great suffering and held firm. Some of you were abused and tormented to make a public show, while others stood loyally by those who were so badly treated. And you had compassion on me in my chains, and cheerfully accepted the seizure of your possessions, knowing that you possessed something more lasting in Heaven. Do not then throw away your confidence, for it carries great reward. Because you need patience, so after you have done the will of GOD, you may receive what He has promised. ...We are not among those who shrink back and are lost; we have the faith to make life our own."

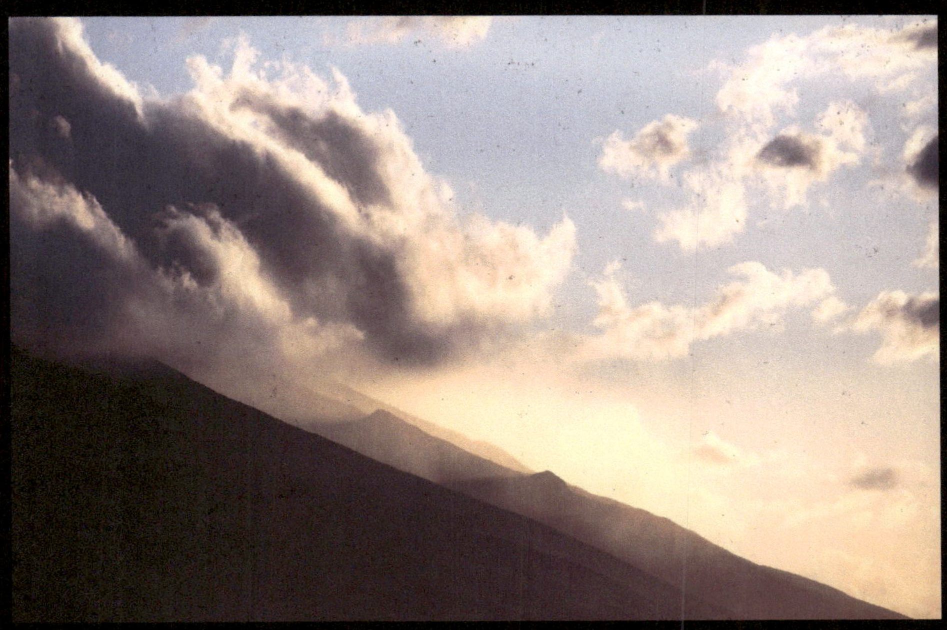

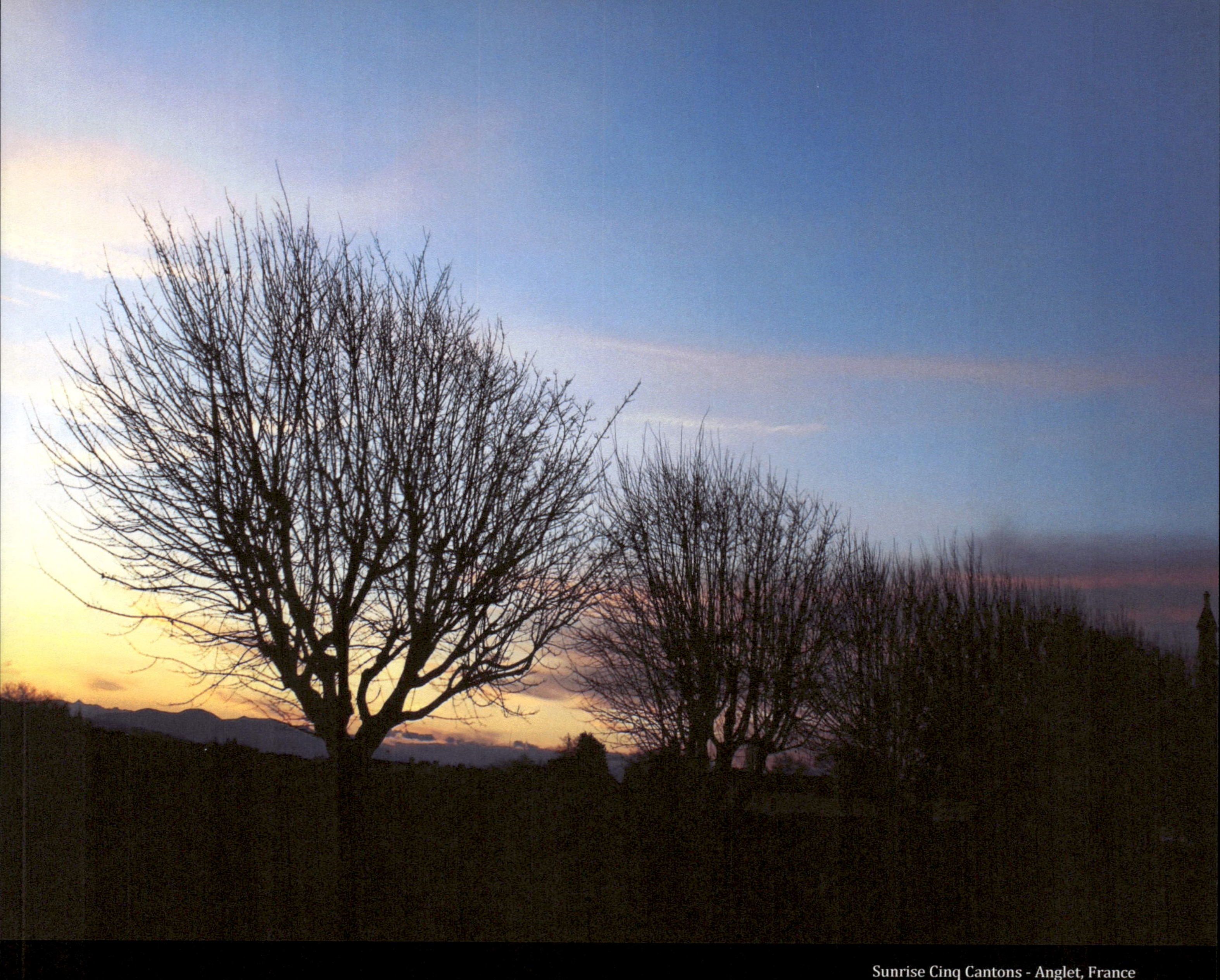

Sunrise Cinq Cantons - Anglet, France

Psalms 27:1

Be fierce, and know that GOD is with you.

"The Lord is my light and my salvation. Whom shall I fear?The LORD is the keeper of my life, so who should I be afraid of? NO one!"

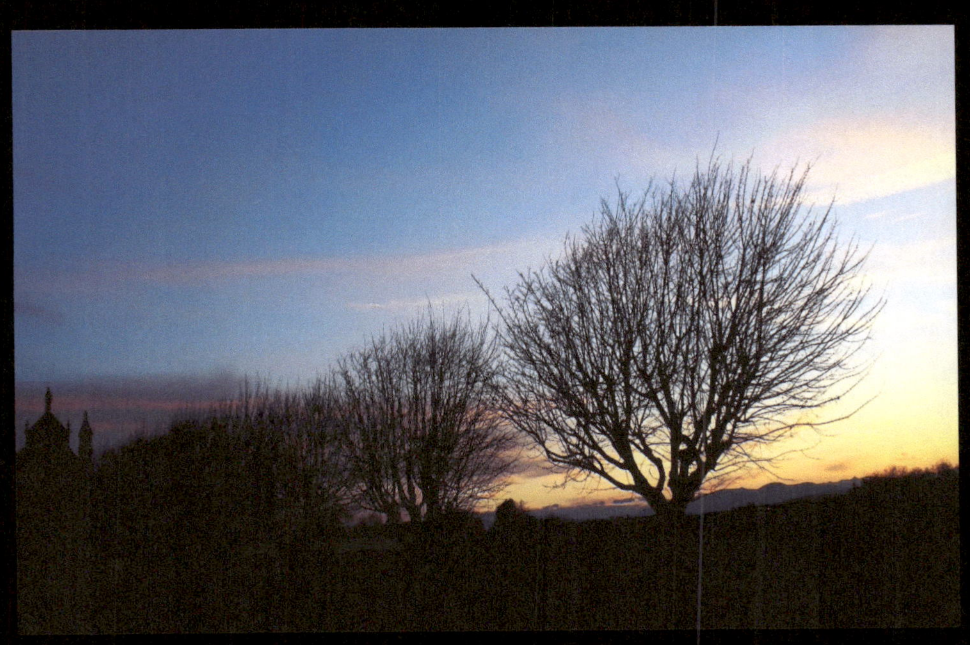

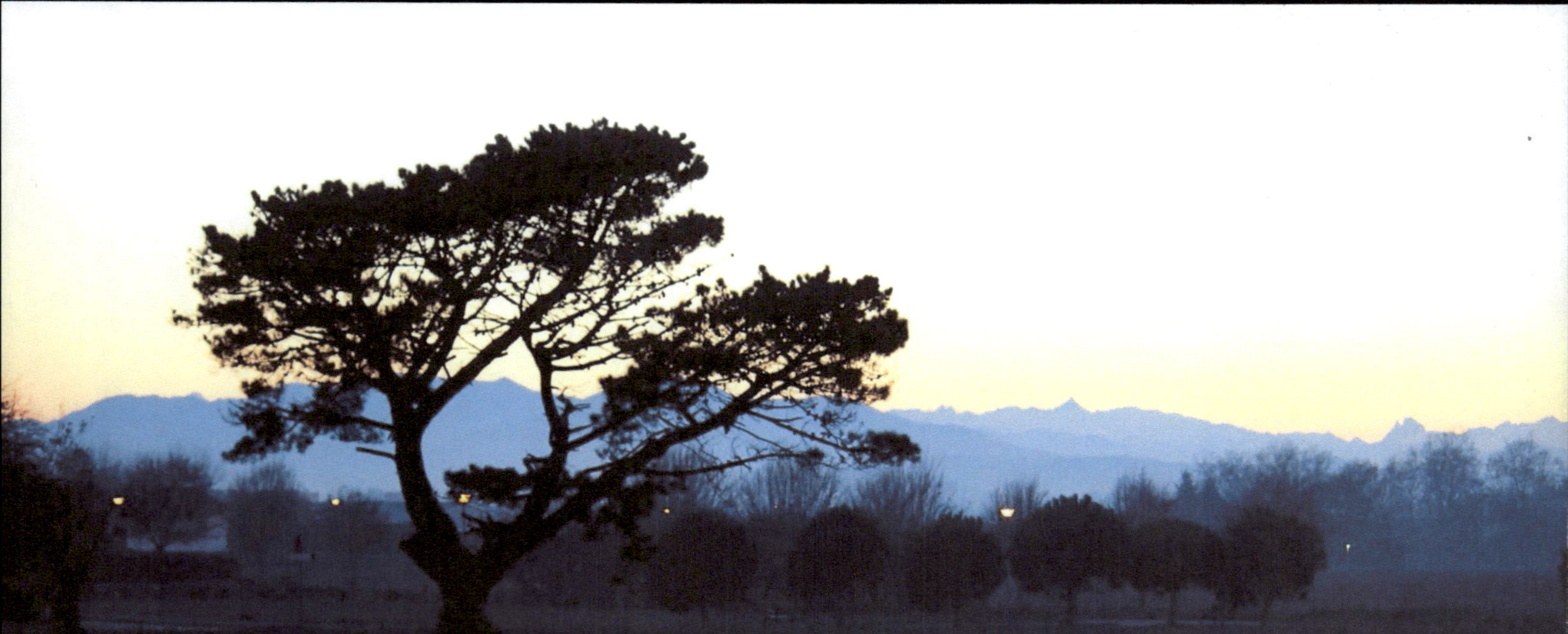

Luke 18:27

Remember: Nothing is impossible for GOD.

Expect miracles.

"Whatever is impossible for men is possible for GOD."

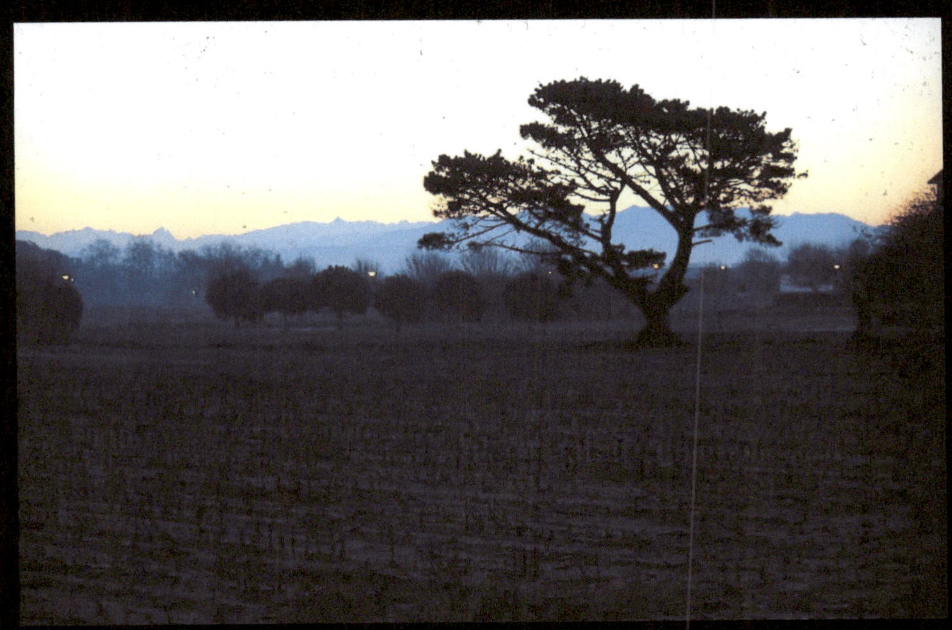

If I can inspire a heart to beat again, or breathe life into a dream;
hearten those who cry in the night and bring them the morning sun,
then my journey was worth the tears, and I triumphed in the midst of them all.
-D. Ashanti-Dubois

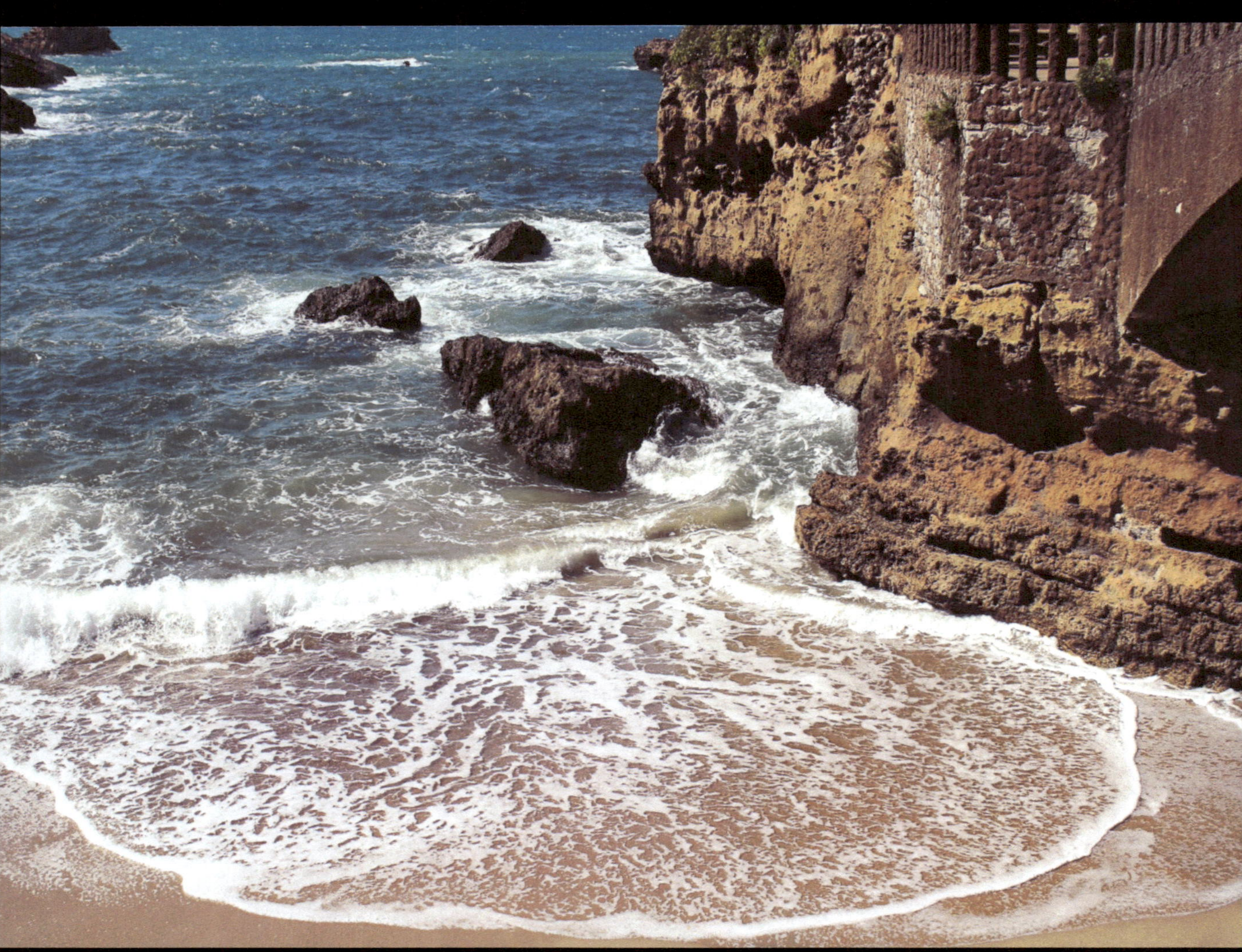

Pays Basque - Biarritz, France

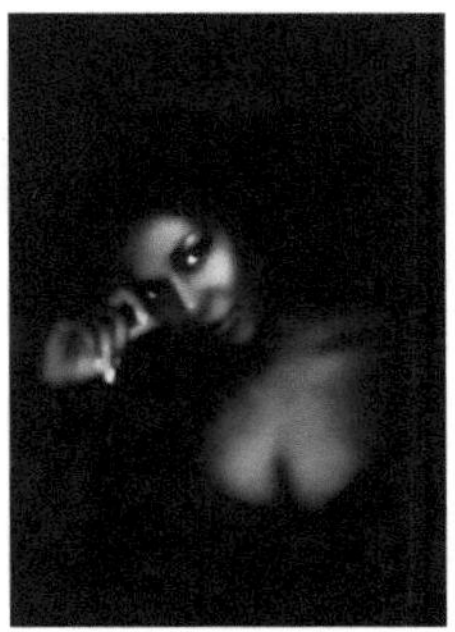

ABOUT THE AUTHOR

Author and creative artist D. Ashanti-Dubois brings light and love to the universe of literature through her latest edition, Messages of Hope – Inspiration From the Holy Bible. As a multifaceted writer, photographer, vocalist, composer, graphiste, and artiste, D. Ashanti-Dubois brings a unique perspective to the world of spiritual enlightenment. After nearly two decades of living internationally and in Hawaii, her many travels have emboldened her belief in the spirit of hope, love, and humanity.

Born and raised in St. Louis, Missouri where she began her creative journey writing poetry, prose, and songs at the tender age of five, D. Ashanti-Dubois continues her artistic odyssey producing various genres of books, music, photography, and art. Her spiritual anthology, *Messages of Hope,* is a collection of beautifully written spiritual insights that will inspire and empower your life. The entire Messages of Hope series can be purchased online through Amazon.com and other vendors.

Also available: *Messages of Hope – Words to Uplift the Human Spirit:* An uplifting book of 33 inspire messages and 36 exercises to heal your life with more than 150 gorgeous original photographs. *Messages d'Amour– Reflections of Love:* A romantic diary of love poems with gorgeous floral photography to inspire love and romance. *Heaven & Earth:* A magnificent collection of spiritual poetry and nature photography.

For more books available by D. Ashanti-Dubois visit www.mydovesong.com. Look for other editions scheduled to be released in the coming years.

www.ingramcontent.com/pod-product-compliance
Lightning Source LLC
LaVergne TN
LVHW070133110826
845147LV00002B/239

9780615977812